club 9 nine

by
MAKOTO KOBAYASHI

translation
DANA LEWIS and TOREN SMITH

lettering and retouch
JASON HVAM

Dark Horse Comics®

publisher
MIKE RICHARDSON

series editors
MIKE HANSEN and TIM ERVIN-GORE

collection editor
CHRIS WARNER

executive editor
TOREN SMITH for STUDIO PROTEUS

collection designer
LANI SCHREIBSTEIN

art director
MARK COX

English-language version produced by
DARK HORSE COMICS and STUDIO PROTEUS

CLUB 9 Volume 1

The artwork of this volume has been produced as a mirror-image of the original Japanese edition to conform to English-language standards.

Published by
Dark Horse Comics, Inc.
10956 SE Main Street
Milwaukie, OR 97222

www.darkhorse.com

To find a comics shop in your area, call the Comic Shop Locator Service
toll-free at 1-888-266-4226

First edition: February 2003
ISBN: 1-56971-915-2

EPISODE 1
HEBA! Y'ALL KIN CALL ME HARUO!
HEBA: JAPANESE AKITA PROVINCIAL DIALECT FOR "HELLO" AND "GOODBYE." THINK OF BOTH "HOWDY" AND "SEE Y'ALL"... WITH "ALOHA" MIXED IN!

1992: THE SUMMER NATIONAL HIGH SCHOOL BASEBALL CHAMPIONSHIPS AT KŌSHIEN STADIUM. HATSUGOYA ACADEMY HIGH SCHOOL BECOMES THE FIRST SCHOOL FROM RURAL AKITA PREFECTURE TO REACH THE PLAYOFFS SINCE 1915...
...AND THEN, MIRACLE OF *MIRACLES,* AKITA'S FIRST *ALL JAPAN CHAMPIONS!*

THE MASS MEDIA GOES WILD OVER HATSUGOYA ACE PITCHER, *KINGORŌ ECHIZENYA.* WILL HE FOLLOW IN THE FOOTSTEPS OF HISASHI YAMADA AND HIROMITSU OCHIAI TO BECOME AKITA'S *THIRD SUPERSTAR* OF THE GAME...?!

WHAT PRO TEAM DO YOU HOPE TO PLAY FOR, KINGORŌ?!
TH' *LIONS* 'R TH' *GIANTS!* I AIN'T SETTLIN' FER ANYTHIN' LESS!
WHAT'S YOUR LIFE DREAM, KINGORŌ?!
ONE O' THEM *FERARRI TESTAROSSA* CARS, JEST LIKE KIYOHARA OF THE LIONS GOT!!

AND THEN... NOVEMBER!
THE PROFESSIONAL DRAFT!

1992 PRO DRAFT COUNCIL
THE FIRST DRAFT PICKS!
新
ラッテ
広島
福岡ユニャー
RUTTE
H
ヤタルト
オラックス
中目
日本ガム
ORAX
中目
読買
近哲
横浜
西部

西部
THE LIONS...
Lions

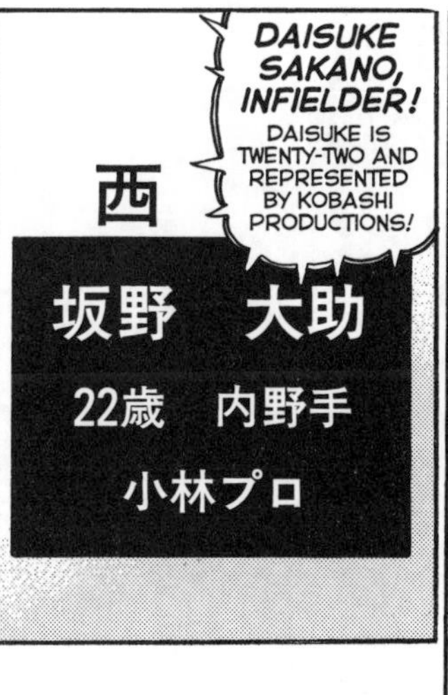
DAISUKE SAKANO, INFIELDER!
DAISUKE IS TWENTY-TWO AND REPRESENTED BY KOBASHI PRODUCTIONS!
西
坂野 大助
22歳 内野手
小林プロ

IT'S A DREAM COME TRUE!
YEE-HAW! THE SEIBU LIONS!
SHARP

.....
.....
AND NEXT, THE GIANTS!!
MICHIAKI KIYAMA, INFIELDER! MICHIYAKI IS EIGHTEEN AND COMES TO THE PROS STRAIGHT FROM THE KANOYA HIGH SCHOOL TEAM!
読　買
木山　道明
18歳　内野手
鹿屋南高校

I CAIN'T B'LIEVE IT! I JUST CAIN'T!!
I'LL PLAY LIKE A HORSE AFIRE, YOU JEST WATCH!
.....
.....

...AND NOW, MOVING INTO THE FOURTH ROUND OF DRAFT PICKS...
SHŌTA FUMIMURA FOR THE SWALLOWS ...
KAZUYUKI SAITŌ FOR THE TIGERS... ....
タルト
翔太
オラックス
下坂　保
中　日
田中　敬三
坂井　裕
買
和男
近　哲
汐崎まこと
横　浜
西　保雄
西　部
山野　勝
--AND THAT BRINGS TO A CLOSE THIS YEAR'S ROOKIE DRAFT PICK COUNCIL. OUR THANKS TO YOU ALL FOR ATTENDING!

.....
.....
.....
.....
.....
.....

UH... UM... -koff-
.... -koff-

WELL... UH... IT LOOKS LIKE YOU WEREN'T CHOSEN BY ANYONE. MAYBE NEXT YEAR, HUH?
ER... ANY COMMENT ...?

....!

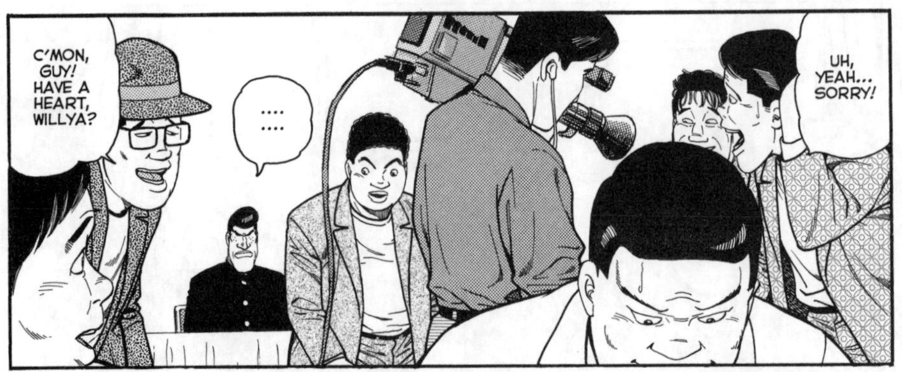
C'MON, GUY! HAVE A HEART, WILLYA?
....
....
UH, YEAH... SORRY!

ACCORDING TO A SCOUT FOR THE BUFFALOES...
OH, THE KID? KINGORŌ ECHIZENYA?
HE PITCHED SOME SMOKERS AT KŌSHIEN, YEAH...
BUT... I DUNNO... FOR A PRO LEAGUE ...?

THE SCOUT FOR THE SWAL-LOWS ...
HIM? NAW. THERE WERE PLENTY OF PLAYERS WE WANTED MORE.
THE GIANTS ...
I'M AFRAID HE JUST DIDN'T FIT INTO OUR LINEUP.
AND THE LIONS ...
HONESTLY, WHO KNOWS WHY THEY WON AT KŌSHIEN? WAS IT REALLY KINGORŌ...

...OR SOMETHING ELSE?

AKITA
PREFECTURE

hahh hff
hahh whew
GOL-LEE! LOOKIT THEM SNOW-FLAKES... BIGGER'N GOOSE FEATHERS!
TOO BAD I GOTTA GET ME A MOVE ON!

AH JEST LOOOOVE SNOW! ♥
SO CLEAN AN' PURE AN' VIRGIN WHITE!
MMM... DON'T Y'ALL NEVER STOP!
TURN TH' WHOLE WIDE WORLD CLEAN AN' WHITE!
♩♩ MAH SWEET SUGAR SNO-- ♩

GBLORSH

送別会
ハツ小屋学園
野球部
さようなら3年生
SIGNS: "FAREWELL PARTY! SAYONARA, SENIOR CLASS! (HATSUGOYA ACADEMY BASEBALL TEAM)"

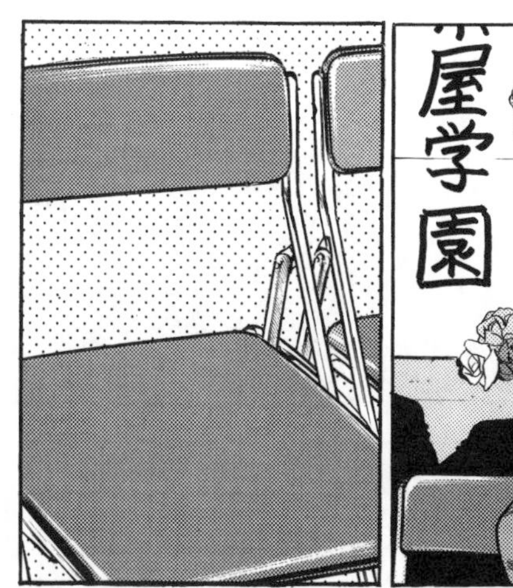

AH SWEAR, THET GIRL IS SLOWER N' COAL TAR RUNNIN' UPHILL ***BACK-WARDS!***
WHY'N BLAZES AIN'T SHE HERE, YET?!

WHADDAYA THINK, KINGORŌ? FIGGER WE OUGHTTA JEST GET THINGS A'ROLLING?
WHOA, ***WHOA!*** HOLD ON THERE!
WHUT'S THE BIG OL' HURRY?

WE JEST CAIN'T START WITHOUT ***HARUO,*** KIN WE?
WE'D STILL BE CHASIN' GROUNDERS INTA FARMER SATO'S PIGPEN INSTEAD A' CLEANING UP AT TH' ***JAPAN CHAMPION-SHIPS*** IFFEN IT WARN'T FER HER BEIN' OUR MANAGER!

AIN'T THAT TH' ***TRUTH!***

MEBBE SHE TRIED RIDIN' HER BIKE IN THIS HERE SNOW OR SOME SUCH OTHER FOOL-ASS HARUO STUNT!
YOU THAR! GIT ALONG AND HAVE A LOOK AROUND IN TH' DITCHES!
YASSIR!

C'MON, Y'ALL! WE GOTS T' HAUL BUGGY FER TOWN!
WHAM
TOWN ...? WHAT'S TH--
IT'S LI'L HARUO!

THEY EVEN DRUG HER OFF T' THE HOSPITAL!
SHE DONE FALLED INTO A CESSPIT AGIN!!

.....!
.....!
.....!

OVER HYAR!
THUD
WHAM

SORRY T' BE IN SUCH A HURRYMENT, MA'AM, BUT Y'ALL GOT A MISSY IN HERE NAME A' HARUO HATTORI!?!
SHORE DO, AN' DON'T WE ALL KNOW IT! JEST FOLLER YER NOSE DOWN T' ROOM 202!

THUD THUD
THET WAY!
HARUO ...!!
WHAM

. . .
. . .

OOO WAA HOO!!
LIKE A DAID SKUNK!
THET'S THE AWFULLEST SMELL AH EVER SMELT!

DON'T BE KILLED DAID, HARUO!
phogh!
THINK ABOUT YER PORE DAD!
HE ALREADY PAID THET BIG CITY UNIVERSITY!
PEE-YOO!!

OOOHH... S... SMELLY ...

AH ...?

SHE WOKED UP! SHE'LL BE RIGHT!!
YUH OKAY, HARUO?!
WE WAS PURT' NEAR WORRIED T' *DEATH!*

OH! DON'T TELL ME YOU *ALL* DONE COME T' SEE ME?

B-BUT... THET MEANS AH RUINT THE PARTY!
AWW, 'TAIN'T NO THANG, HARUO!

HOLD ON A MITE!
PARTY'S WHERE TH' FOLKS ARE, AND TH' GANG'S ALL *HERE,* AIN'T THEY?!
AH'LL GO GIT THE FIXIN'S!

MISS HARUO, YOU IS BEEN TH' BEST MANAGER WE *EVER* HAD AN' THAT'S TH' PURE TRUTH!!
WE IS *BUSTIN'* PROUD YOU IS GOIN' OFF TO TOKYO TO THAT FANCY UNIVERSITY, BUT DON'T YUH FERGIT US, Y'HEAR?

LOOKY! WE WORKED ON THIS OF AN EV'NIN' ALL LAST MONTH!
IT'LL KEEP YUH WARM AS A JUNE BRIDE IN A FEATHER BED! ♥

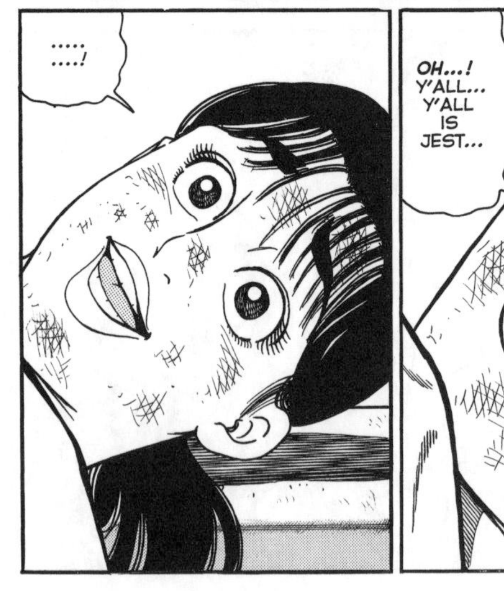
....., ...!

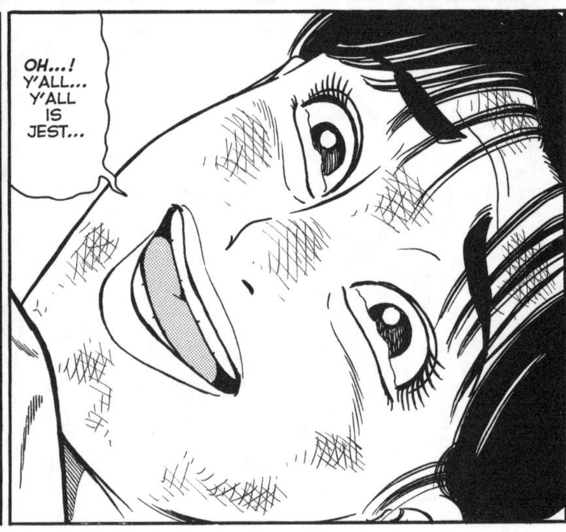
OH...! Y'ALL... Y'ALL IS JEST...

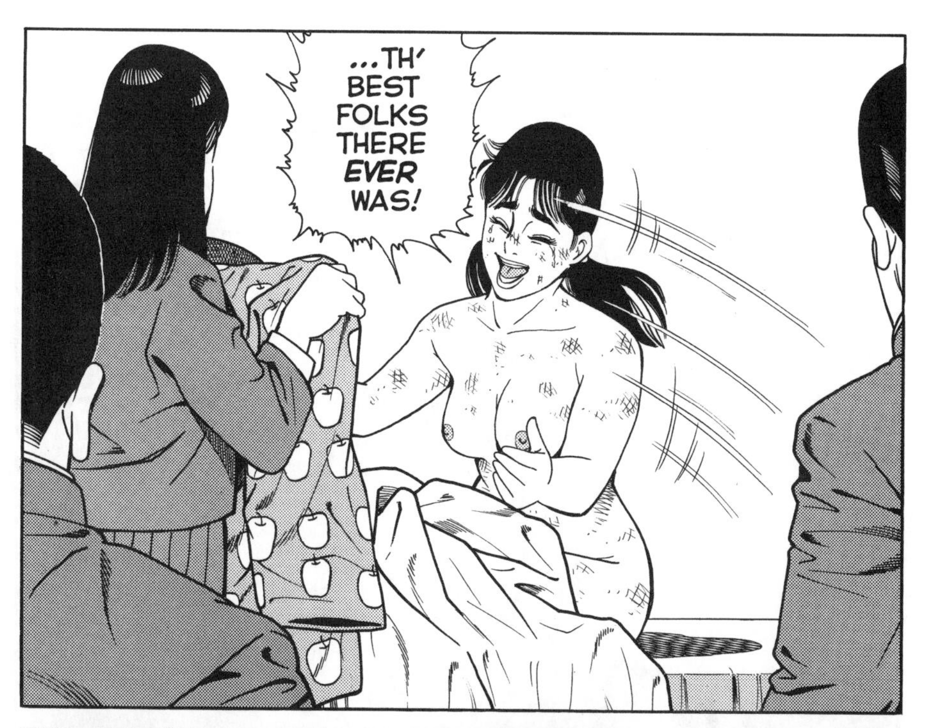

HEBA!
Y'ALL KIN CALL ME
HARUO!

MY HIGH SCHOOL DAYS WAS A PURE, PURE PLEASURE, BUT NOW I GOT TO MOVE ON DOWN TO TOKYO TO FINISH UP MY BOOK LEARNING!
MY PLANS? I'M FIXING TO STUDY LIKE A TREE FULL OF OWLS FOR FOUR YEARS, THEN I'M HIGHTAILING IT BACK HOME HERE TO AKITA TO BE A SCHOOL-TEACHER! ♥

EPISODE 2
THE VOW

HOLY CAT-FISH!
GRANNY ...!
TAKE CARE BEHIND YUH, NOW!

....

HAW...??

WATCH YER TAIL FEATHERS!
IT'S STEEPER N' STRAIGHT UP BEHIND YUH!

.....
.....

HAW...??

BEHIND YUH, GRANNY!
I SAID TAKE CARE BEHIND YUH!

HAW ...??

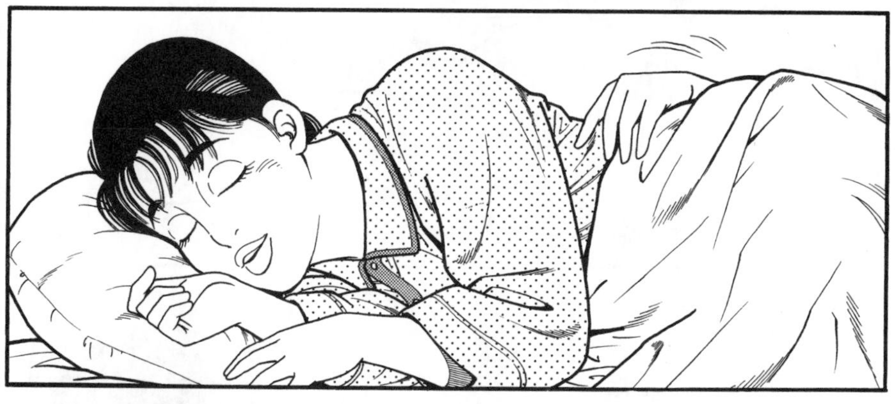

mmm... DARLIN', YOU SURELY IS ALLLL GROWED UP NOW.
AH ...?

OH, MOMMA!

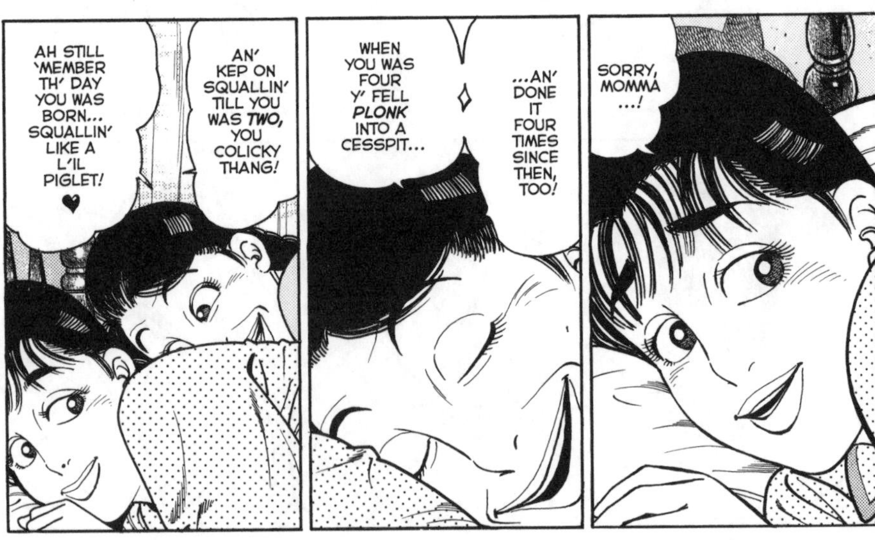
AH STILL 'MEMBER TH' DAY YOU WAS BORN... SQUALLIN' LIKE A L'IL PIGLET! ♥
AN' KEP ON SQUALLIN' TILL YOU WAS TWO, YOU COLICKY THANG!
WHEN YOU WAS FOUR Y' FELL PLONK INTO A CESSPIT...
...AN' DONE IT FOUR TIMES SINCE THEN, TOO!
SORRY, MOMMA ...!

AN' NOW... EIGHTEEN!
TH' BEST TIMES OF YORE LIFE.

FER THE NEXT COUPLE O' YEARS YOU'LL BE TH' HONEY...
...AND TH' BEES'LL ALL KNOW IT!

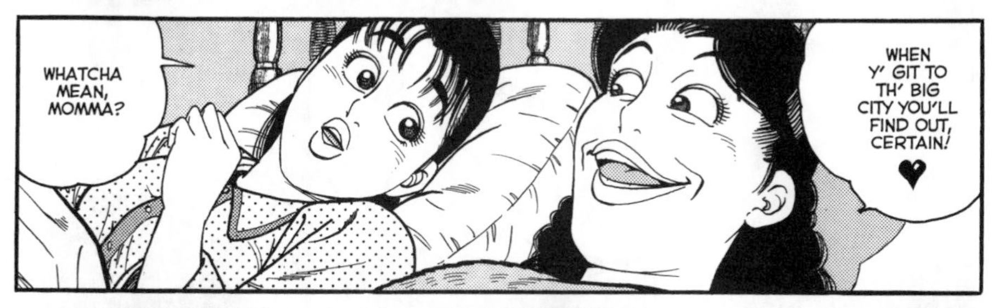
WHATCHA MEAN, MOMMA?
WHEN Y' GIT TO TH' BIG CITY YOU'LL FIND OUT, CERTAIN! ♥

BUT YER PORE OL' MOMMA...
...IN JEST SEVENNY-NINE MORE DAYS...

...SH-SHE'S A' GONNA BE... .....

.....
.....

.....
....?

WAAAHH!!
LORDY, MOMMA! WHAT YOU ALL FLUSTERATED ABOUT?!

WHUT'S THE HUBBUB?
KCHAK

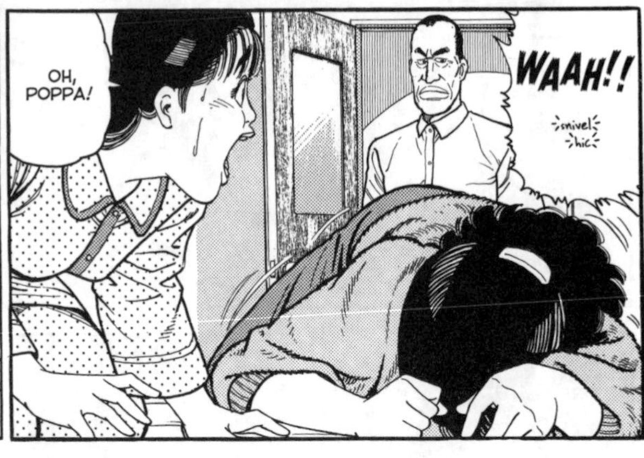
OH, POPPA!
WAAH!!
snivel
hic

IT... IT'S JEST ...
...MOMMA DON'T WANT T' TURN FORTY!

EVERYONE TURNS FORTY ONE DAY, MOMMA-- IFFEN THEY MAKE IT!
YER JEST ADDIN' ONE L'IL OL' YEAR TO THIRTY-NINE!
I HATE IT I HATE IT I HATE IT! FORTY!
WAAH!!
Y'ALL MIGHT AS WELL JEST CHOP UP MAH WRINKLED OLE BUTT AN' FEED ME TO THE HAWGS!!

.....
.....

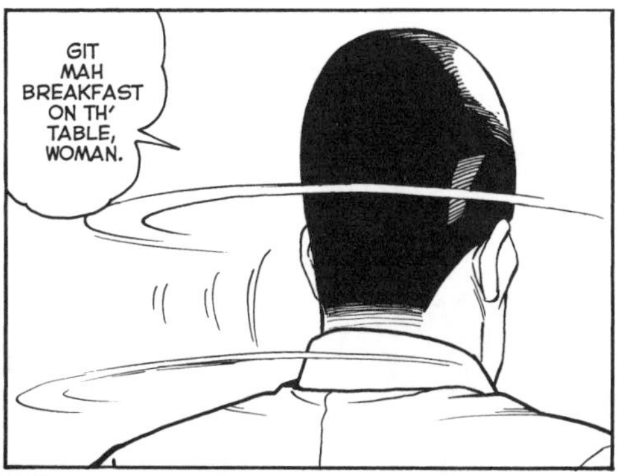
GIT MAH BREAKFAST ON TH' TABLE, WOMAN.

IT'S FRIDAY THE 29TH...
...AND WELCOME TO... MORNING ANGLE!!
I'M YOUR HOST, IEJIRŌ TOKUGAWA!

OUR FIRST NEWS ITEM...
LA LA LALA LAA LAA!
LIKE A VIR-GIN ...!

POPPA ...?

.....
.....

UM... NOW, I KNOW MAH POPPA IS GONNA MISS HIS L'IL GIRL...
...BUT I'LL COME BACK EVER' VACATION, AH PROMISE!

.....
.....

HARUO.

YES, POPPA ?!

NOW... LISTEN HYAR... WHEN YER OFF IN TH' BIG CITY...
LA-LA LAA LAH!!
LA LA LALA LAA LAA!
...I WANT YUH T' BE CAREFUL, Y'HEAR? A YOUNG LADY SECH AS YER--
LAA! LAA!
FAK FAK
LIKE A VIRRR... IRR... IRRRGIN!
.....
.....

NOW, YOU STAY OUTTA TH' HENHOUSE, Y'OLD HOUND DOG, YOU! ♥
WUFF! WURF!
犬注意 かみつきます!!
マルの家
SIGN: "BEWARE OF THE DOG! HE BITES!"

I'LL COME BACK AN' SEE YUH EVER' VACATION, AH PROMISE!
HEBA!
whiiine!
hahh hahh

GRR!!
Oomph!!

FWHSSH

WUFFA!
Maruuu!!
GIMME BACK MAH BEST TRAVELIN' SKIRT RAHT NOW!!
WHY YOU MANGY LITTLE POT LICKER!!

YUH BETTER GET A HUMP ON OR WE'RE GONNA MISS YER PLANE!
WHY YOU ALWAYS LOLLYGAGGIN' AROUND, GIRL?!

I'M HEADING OUT OF MY HOMETOWN FOR THE FIRST TIME IN MY WHOLE LIFE! FOR UNIVERSITY IN THE BIG CITY!
MY NAME IS HARUO HATTORI, AND I'M JUST A PLAIN OLD COUNTRY GIRL.
SORRY, PA!

NOW, JUST BEFORE
I LEFT FOR TOKYO,
I MADE ME A SOLEMN,
"CROSS MY HEART
AN' HOPE TO DIE" VOW.
VRMMMBB

WHAT KIND
OF VOW, Y'ALL
WANT TO
KNOW...?
VWHOOSH
AKITA
AIRPORT

NOW, HARUO... AS I WAS SAYIN', YOU BE *RIGHT CAREFUL,* Y'HEAH?! TOKYO'S FULL O'--
LOTS O' MIGHTY TASTY YOUNG FELLERS! ♥
非常口
EXIT
I'LL BE JEST *FINE,* Y'ALL!
THAT THERE DORM IS SUPERVISED AN' ALL STRICT AN' SUCH!

AND B'SIDES, I MADE ME A *SPECIAL* VOW! ♥

THAT A FACT ...?
TELL YER OLD PA.

CAIN'T! I KIN ONLY TELL *MOMMA!*
....
....

.....
.....
.....
.....
HEE HEE HEE!
Y'ALL TAKE CARE NOW, POPPA, MOMMA!
AH'LL CALL YUH IFFEN AH HAVE EVEN A *SPECK* O' TROUBLE! **HEBA!!**

VWHOOOSH

WHOOOSHH

AW RIGHT. WHUT KINDA VOW?
MM?
JEST A LI'L OLE PROMISE SHE CAIN'T ***NEVER*** KEEP! ♥

THE BASEBALL SEASON OPENED TODAY WITH A BANG!
プロ野球ワイド
LET'S START WITH THAT RED-HOT SHOWDOWN BETWEEN THE GIANTS AND THE SEIBU LIONS!

LAST YEAR, THE ACE SEIBU LIONS PITCHER KŌJI URYŪ FINISHED THE SEASON WITH NINETEEN WINS AND A RECORD TEN MILLION YEN CONTRACT!
おもちゃの キッキー木山
合田建設
SEIBU
AND TODAY HE KICKED OFF THE SEASON WITH A SLICK PERFORMANCE, ALLOWING NO RUNS, NO HITS IN THREE INNINGS.

YOU SURE POLISHED THEM OFF TODAY, KŌJI, BUT WHAT'S YOUR GOAL THIS YEAR?!
DON'T TELL ME-- TWENTY WINS?!
YEAH, THAT'S ONE OF THEM, BUT...

...I FIGURE THIS YEAR IT'S TIME TO FIND MYSELF A WIFE! HAW HAW!
VRMMMM

VRMMMM
What's Bear? 1
ayashi
Writer and Artist:
Makoto Konbayashi
...?

......!

"HEBA!!
HARUO!"

KINGORŌ!!

AH'LL BE WAITIN' HERE FER YUH, HARUO! FER ALL THEM YEARS!!

MEBBE AH DIN'T MAKE IT INTA THEM PRO LEAGUES.
BUT WHILE I WAS PLAYIN' MY HEART OUT JEST TO SEE YER SMILE...
...WE WON TH' CHAMPIONSHIP AT KŌSHIEN!!

BY TH' TIME YUH COME ON BACK T' STAY, HARUO, THIS MUDDY OL' RICE FIELD IS GONNA BE GROWIN' THE BEST DAMN APPLES IN ALL OF JAPAN!!
SO I, KINGORŌ ECHIZENYA, VOW T' MAKE MYSELF A WINNER AGAIN... ON THIS HERE NEW PLAYIN' FIELD!!

SO YOU WAIT FER ME!
I'LL STUDY 'TIL MAH BRAIN'S FIT T' BUST AND I WON'T NEVER FAIL, HONEY!

FER FOUR LONG YEARS... UNTIL AH COME HOME T' AKITA FER GOOD...
'CAUSE JEST FER MAH DARLIN' KINGORŌ...
...AH MADE ME A VOW!

...AH SWEAR T' STAY A VIRGIN!!

EPISODE 3
YOU KNOW WHAT THEY SAY
ABOUT TOKYO...

POLICE REPORT THEY STILL HAVE NO LEADS IN LAST NIGHT'S *SHOCKING MURDER* NEAR TOKYO'S FUKAZAWA COLLEGE. THE VICTIM, A COLLEGE COED LIVING ALONE, WAS FOUND NAKED AND STRANGLED IN HER APARTMENT WITH CRYPTIC DESIGNS SCRAWLED ON HER BREASTS IN BLACK MARKER PEN.

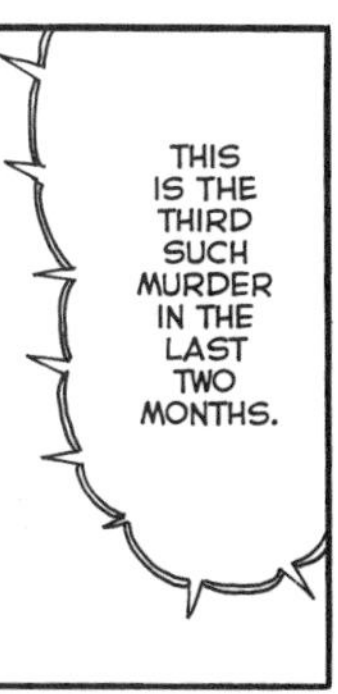
THIS IS THE THIRD SUCH MURDER IN THE LAST TWO MONTHS.

....
....
A POLICE SPOKESMAN SAYS UNTIL THE PERPETRATOR IS CAUGHT, THEY RECOMMEND FEMALE UNIVERSITY STUDENTS TAKE SPECIAL PRECAUTIONS.

WHO MIGHT HAVE COM-MITTED THIS HEINOUS CRIME *...?*
FOR THAT, WE TURN TO A SPECIALIST IN CRIMINAL PSYCHOLOGY, PROFESSOR *MICHIO HINO.*

FIRST, WE MAY PRESUME THAT THE PERPETRATOR WAS A VICTIM OF SEXUAL ABUSE IN HIS PRE-ADOLESCENCE.
SECOND, HIS PERVERTED DESIRE FOR *COLLEGE COEDS* MAY STEM FROM REJECTION BY SAME, OR POSSIBLY *IMPOTENCE!*

....
....!
....
....
I FEAR IT IS ALL TOO LIKELY THIS TORTURED SOUL WILL GO ON TO KILL AGAIN... AND *AGAIN!!*

BWA HAW HAW HAW!!
LOOKIT HIS HAYR, PA!
LOOKS LAIK A ROLL A' BOB WIRE!
.....
.....

WHHOOSSH
YAMANOTE LINE
JR

NOT TOO CROWDED?
UH-UH... I'M *FINE.*
KTAKK KTAKK KTAKK

SHINJUKU STATION NEXT! SHINJUKU!!
RMMMBBB
EEEK!!
RMBB
AHH! MIKI!

OWWEE!
umph!
RMBBB

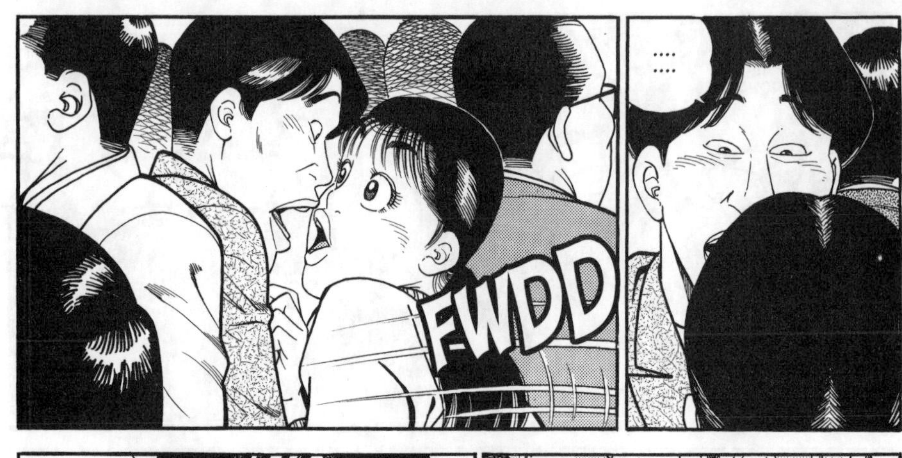
FWDD
....
....

AH... AH'M SORRY, MISTER!

....
....

....
...!
HEH... NO PROB, MISS!

SIGN: SHIBUYA STATION
JR
渋谷駅
"Poppa? Momma? Are you all doing okay? How's Maru?

"I know it's been two whole weeks since I came to Tokyo and got me set up at Fukazawa College, and this is my first letter to you all, but...
"... I've been real busy with classes and orientation and meetings and such, but now things are settling down a mite. I already made me a passel of friends, and mostly I'm happy as a hog in slops!
海外でマスター

深沢学院

HUH
...?

HARUO
...?
HARUO! IS THET YOU?!

EH
...?

AAHH?!
KEN
...?

WALL, I'LL BE!! I AIN'T SEEN YOU SINCE GRAD-DYATION!
FEELS LAIK A DAWG'S AGE AGO, DON'T IT?!
HECK, I FIGGERED WE'D RUN ACROST EACH OTHER SOMETIME, GOING TO TH' SAME SCHOOL AND ALL!
YER LOOKIN' FULL O' BEANS!

THANK'EE! SO--WHUT POSITION THEY GOT YOU ON IN TH' BASEBALL TEAM...?

WELL, NOW
...
FACT IS, I AIN'T EVEN TRIED OUT.

EH ...?!

HAW, HAW, HAW!
WHUT TH--?! BUT THET'S WHY YUH CAME ON **DOWN** HERE! T' JOIN TH' COLLEGE TEAM, THEN GO **PRO!!**

NOT WHEN IT WAS **YER** HOME RUN THET PUT US AHEAD! YOU AIN'T **NEVER** BEEN SHUT OUT!
DON'T YOU TALK LAIK A PLUMB FOOL, KENJI NAKAMURA!
THET'S TRUE, BUT... THINKIN' ABOUT IT, IT JEST DON'T MAKE NO SENSE THAT WE WON AT KŌSHIEN.

SO I'M GETTING' ME A PART-TIME **JOB,** AND SAVIN' UP SOME CASH MONEY--GONNA BUY' ME A **CAR!**
WALL, MEBBE SO. BUT ANYHOW, I NEVER DID **NOTHIN'** BUT PLAY BASEBALL BACK IN AKITA, AND NOW I WANTS T' HAVE ME A BIT O' FUN!! THIS HERE IS **TOKYO,** RIGHT?!

Y'KNOW WHAT MAH DARLIN' KINGORŌ USED T' TELL ME? "THET DAMN NAKAMURA, HE AIN'T LIKE ME! I JEST PRACTICE MAH BRAINS OUT, BUT THAT OL' BOY... HE'S PLAIN GOT BASEBALL IN HIS **BLOOD!"**
I DUNNO, KEN.

HUH...? KINGORŌ SAID **THET...?**

VRMBB

EHH ...?! THAT THANG?
AIN'T TOKYO SOMETHIN'...? YER'D NEVER SEE ONE O' THEM IN AKITA!
WHOA, NELLY!! LOOKIT THET!! A FAH-RARI TESTA-ROH-SA!!

IT'S PIG-BITIN' UGLY!
DON'T Y' TRY T' TELL ME THET'S S'POSE T'BE COOL!

NOW, ME... AH LAIK THIS LI'L CUTIE HEAH!
WHUT'S THIS ONE CALLED?
HAW, HAW... THAT THERE PUDDLE-JUMPER'S A "TODAY" ...!
AH?! LORDY, I'M GONNA BE LATE!!
AH'M IN TH' WOMEN'S DORM BUILDIN' NUMBER FOUR. DON'T BE A STRANGER, Y'HEAH?
HEBA!!
HEH... THERE SURELY IS SOMETHIN' SPECIAL ABOUT THAT GAL.
OHMPH!
....
...!
IT'S A PUZZLER HOW A SWEET LI'L THANG LIKE HER...
...ENDED UP WITH A BIG OL' GOON LIKE KIN-GORŌ...

BOOM

BA-
BOOM

BOOM BA-BOOM
BOOM
BOOM

は
入れへ
SNIK

たばこは
吸殻入れへ
What's Bear?
TRASH

1
What's Bear?

.....
.....

HOW MANY TIMES HAVE YOU READ THAT SILLY COMIC, HARUO?
What's Bear?

HUH ...?
AH! AKI, HON!!
What's Bear?
'BOUT A JILLION TIMES! ♥ IT'S 'CAUSE BACK HOME DOWN ON TH' FARM WE GOT US A DAWG WHAT LOOKS JEST LIKE BEAR!
SO WHENEVER AH GETS T' FEELING A BIT HOMESICK, I READ IT AN' THINK 'BOUT MA AND PA AN' MARU!
1 What's Bear?
NO KID-DING. HEH.

I'LL HAVE TO REMEMBER TO TELL MAKO THAT.
HE'LL GET A KICK OUT OF IT.

"MAKO" ...?
WHO'S THET?
.....
.....

THE GUY WHO DOES THAT COMIC.
MAKO-TO KONBAYASHI... GET IT?

EH ...?!

EEK! AKI! YOU *KNOW* MAKOTO KONBAYASHI?!
YEAH. NICE GUY.

PLEASE, AKI! *PLEASE!*
TH' NEXT TIME Y'SEE MISTER KONBAYASHI, CAN YUH GET HIM T' SIGN ME A BOOK?!
AN' KIN YUH ASK HIM T' SIGN IT *"FOR MARU"*...?!
HA HA! HARUO, YOU ARE SUCH A *SCREAM!*
SURE! I'LL ASK HIM, NO PROB.

HUSH *PUPPIES!!* ♥
AH'M *ALL OVER* HAPPY!

AH ...?

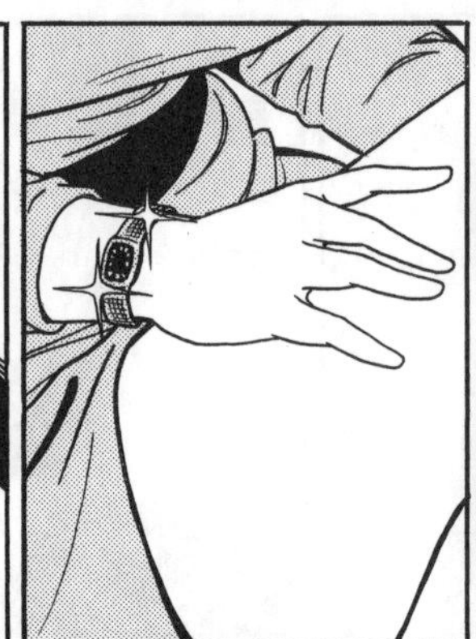

....
....

GOSH, AKI... THAT THERE'S A BEAUTIFUL WATCH!
OH, THIS OLD THING?
IT WAS A PRESENT FROM TOMMY.

"TOMMY" ...? WHO'S THET?

TOMMY HAJIME, GIRL! DON'T YOU KNOW HIM?
THE GUY ON TV!

WHAT?! THE FELLER ON THEM FUNNY TOILET COMMERCIALS?!
THAT'S HIM!
HE DROPS BY THE PLACE I WORK ALL THE TIME, IN THOSE HORRIBLE-LOOKING SHIRTS HE WEARS! ♥

WOWEE, AKI!
ER... WHAT KINDA WORK D' YOU DO, ANYHOW?
....
....
....
....
....
....

NOT SOMETHING YOU COULD DO, THAT'S FOR SURE.
HEY! THET SOME KINDA INSULT OR SOMETHIN' ...?!
'SIDES, I CAIN'T WORK! 'TAIN'T ALLOWED IF YER STAYIN' IN TH' DORMS!

TELL ME YOU'RE NOT IN BUILDING NUMBER FOUR?
WULL... ACTUALLY ...WHY?

I'M AMAZED YOU CAN STAND IT, GIRL-FRIEND.
IF I WERE YOU, I'D FIND MYSELF SOME PART-TIME WORK AND GET MY OWN PLACE PRONTO!!

AW, 'TAIN'T SO BAD!
IT'S REAL STRICT AN' ALL, BUT AH DON'T MUCH MIND THAT!

YEAH, RULES WERE MADE TO BE BROKEN, HUH?
BUT I MEAN THE OTHER THING!

W-WHAT "OTHER THANG"...?

THE GHOST !!

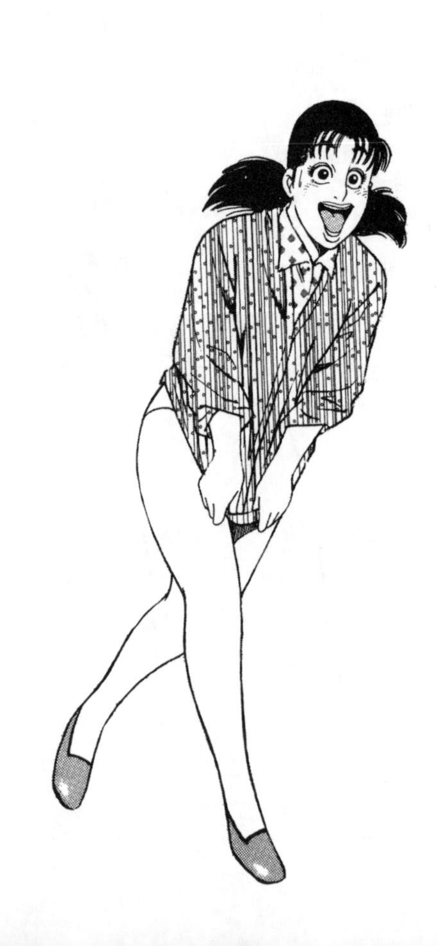

Lions
EPISODE 4
EEEEEEK!!

深沢第一女子寮
SIGN: GIRL'S DORM

IT... IT JEST *CAIN'T* BE TRUE.

THET.... THET THIS HERE DORM USED T'BE A *HOSPITAL MORGUE...*

...AN' THIS HERE BATH WAS WHERE THEY...
...THEY W-WASHED TH' DAID BODIES!

....
....
KSSHH
KSSHH
KSSHH
....
....

BLSSH
....
....!

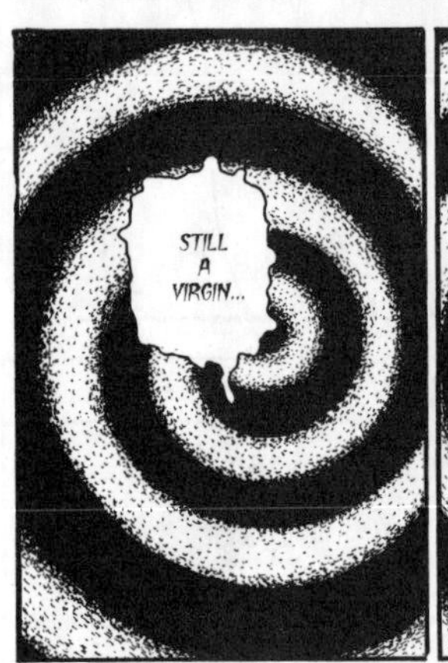
STILL A VIRGIN...

STILL A VIRGIN...

DEAD... AND STILL A VIRGIN!!

NNNNN
hahh
hahh

AH?!

hahh
hahh

...??
hff

....
....

STILL A VIRGIN...

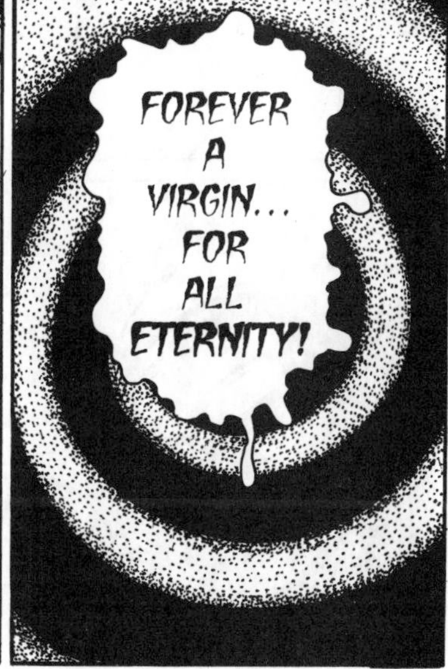
FOREVER A VIRGIN... FOR ALL ETERNITY!

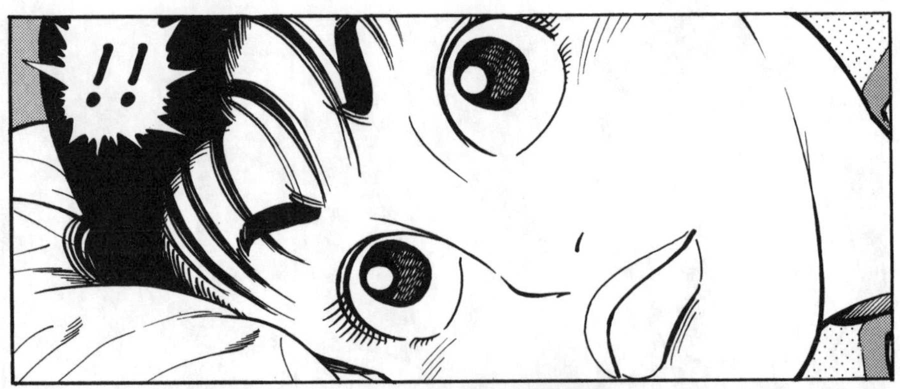

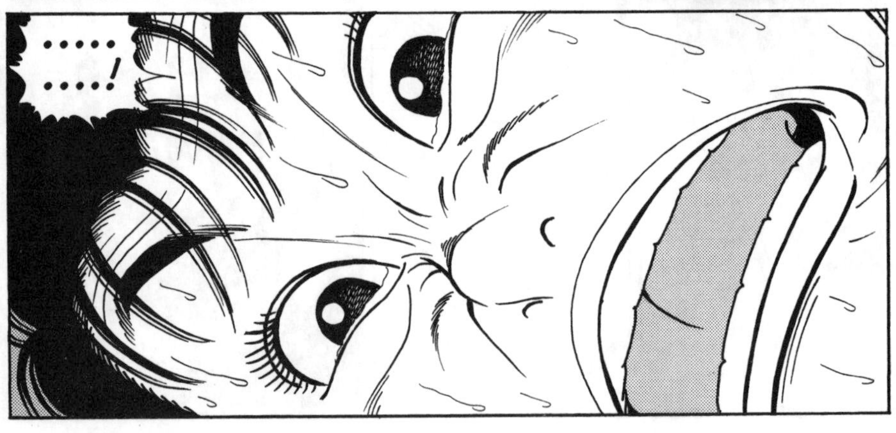

EEEEK!!
WHAT THE HELL IS GOING ON? IT'S THE MIDDLE OF THE GODDAMN NIGHT!
HEY!! DO YOU KNOW WHAT TIME IT IS?!
GEEZ!!

AH SAW IT!!
AH SWEAR I SAW IT!!
FHWUDD
THIS HYAR PLACE REALLY DO GOT A GHOST!!

OOH! YOU SAW THE GHOST?!
I JUST HAD THAT ROOM EXORCISED AGAIN, TOO-- DARN IT!
THAT WORTHLESS PRIEST! DO YOU KNOW WHAT HE CHARGED US?!
AIN'T THERE SOMETHIN' YOU KIN DO, MA'AM?!
DON'T MAKE NO NEVER MIND T' ME WHAR I STAY!
CAIN'T YUH JEST MOVE ME INTA ANOTHER ROOM?!
SORRY, DEAR! THE WAITING LIST IS MILES LONG!
BUT IF YOU WAIT A YEAR, THE SENIORS WILL GRADUATE AND YOU CAN SWITCH. UNTIL THEN, WHY DON'T YOU JUST TRY TO GET ALONG WITH HIM, OKAY?
SO FAR HE SEEMS TO BE PRETTY HARMLESS!

Y-YUH CAIN'T BE SERIOUS ...?!

WHUT ...?!
Y' SAW A GHOST?!

ANYHOW, WE GOT OUR OWN PROBLEMS 'ROUND HERE.
STUFF AN' NONSENSE, GIRL.

WHAT KIND'A PROBLEMS Y'ALL GOT?
HUH? WHAT'S WRONG, PA?!

IT'S YER MA.
SHE DON'T WANT T' TURN FORTY--SHE'S PLUMB OUTTA CONTROL.

SHE'S TRYIN' ALL KINDS O' CRAZY STUFF T' GET ME T' BUY HER A FUR COAT!
♫♩ LIKE A VIRRR...♩ IRRR... GIN!! ♩ ♫

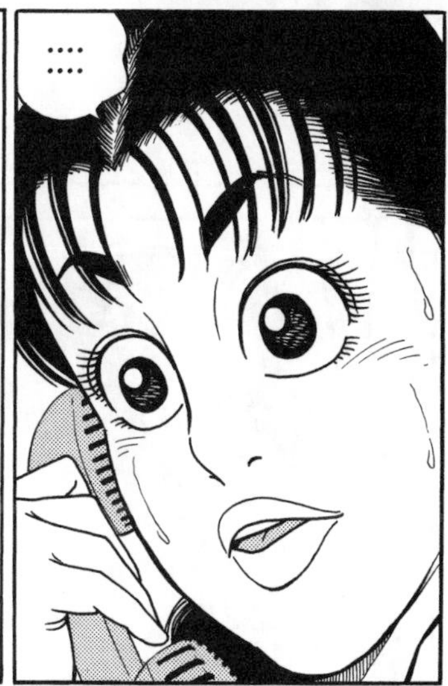
....

Father Sendō Nagareyama
Father Sendō Nagareyama's
EXORCISM FOR DUMMIES
EXORCISM FOR DUMMI

STUDYING THAT OLD BOOK WON'T GET YOU ANYWHERE, KIDDO.
GIVE IT UP!

FUYUMI ...?
Father Sendo Nagareyama's EXORCISM FOR DUMMIES

I'M TELLING YOU-- JUST MOVE OUT!
I'LL GIVE YOU A HAND, GO WITH YOU AND STUFF.
I KNOW SOME AREAS THAT AREN'T TOO BAD!

HEY, NOW YOU "GIVE IT UP" ...!
TOKYO RENTS ARE WAY OUTTA MAH LEAGUE!

SO GET A PART-TIME JOB!
C'MON, HARUO! WE CAN GET A JOB WORKING TOGETHER WITH AKI!
SHE TALKED ME INTO TRYING OUT AT HER PLACE, SO I GAVE IT A SHOT FOR JUST ONE NIGHT, AND...
...IT WAS A GAS! SO MUCH FUN! ♥

B-BUT... AKI SAID I WEREN'T CUT OUT FOR HER KIND'A JOB...
AW, GIMME A BREAK!
YOU'RE *YOUNG!* YOU'RE *FUN!* THAT'S ALL YOU *REALLY* NEED!
OOH! ♥
RYŌJI WAS SUCH A *DREAM-BOAT!!*
HE *LOOKS* STUCK-UP, BUT HE'S REALLY *TOO SWEET!!*

"RYŌJI" ...? WHO'S THET?
RYŌJI ONIZUKA! YOU KNOW-- THE *MOVIE STAR!!*
HE SAT RIGHT *NEXT* TO ME!
EEEK!
I THOUGHT I'D HAVE A *HEART ATTACK!!*

....
....
WE TALKED AND STUFF AND HE SAID I'D MAKE A *PERFECT* WIFE!
AHH!! I WONDER WHEN HE'LL BE *BACK* FOR ME, MY *RYŌJI!!* ♥
EXORCISM FOR DUMMIES
AH AIN'T GOT TH' *TAHM* NOR THE *INCLINATION* RAHT NOW FOR MIXIN' WITH *MENFOLK!*
EXORCISM FOR

I JUMPED INTO THE OCEAN TO SAVE A DROWNING KID, AND INSTEAD, I DROWNED **MYSELF...**

AH KNOW, AH KNOW... YOU DONE TOLT ME 'BOUT A *JILLION* TIMES. YER *SUCH* A HERO.

BUT... I WAS STILL A **VIRGIN!!**

NOW I CAN'T REST IN PEACE!
'TAIN'T NO BUSINESS O' MINE!
IFFEN YER DAID... YER DAID! GIT USED T' IT!
THEN I'LL REST IN PEACE AND LEAVE THIS MORTAL PLANE!
JUST HAVE SEX WITH ME ONCE!!
PLEASE !!

I CANNOT LEAVE THIS PLACE WHILE I AM STILL A VIRGIN!!
I BEG YOU!
I BEG YOU!
hmph!
AN' AH AIN'T PLANNIN' T' GIVE IT UP T' NO CREEPY OL' HAUNT!
AH'LL HAVE YEW KNOW, SIR, AH'M STILL A VIRGIN TOO!!

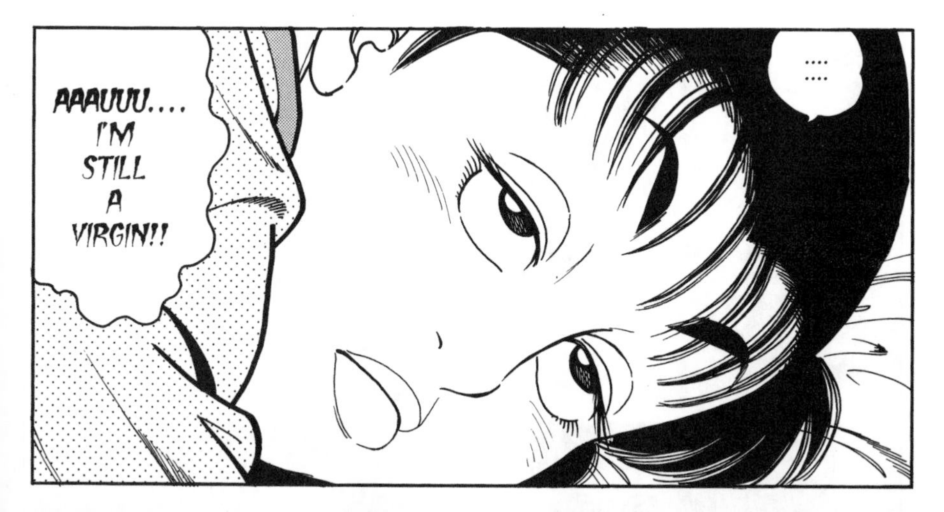
AAAUUU....
I'M STILL A VIRGIN!!
....
....

HEY, KID-- WHAT'S UP?

....
....

UH-OH!
....
....!

THET *GHOST...* -snff-
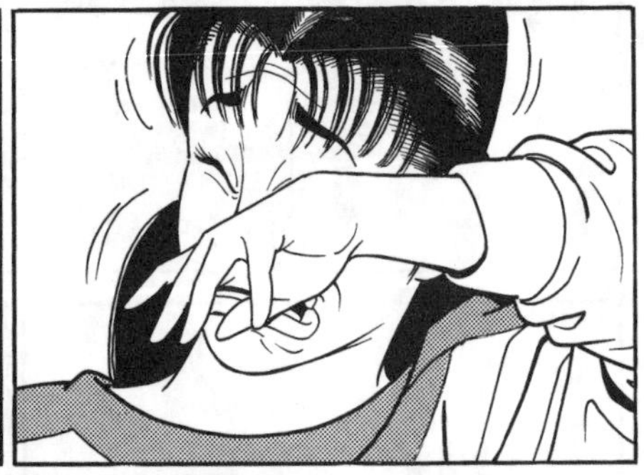

EVER' NIGHT... HE... HE JEST FLOATS THAR, RAHT IN FRONT O' ME, AN'... AN'... -snff-
AN' HE *PULLS* HIS *PUD!!*

.....
.....!
.....
.....!

-snff!-
-snrk!-

THAT DOES IT...!
NO MORE CRYING.

TODAY YOU'RE MOVING IN WITH BIG SISTER AKI!
THERE YOU GO, HARUO! BEATS THE HELL OUT OF SEEING SOME GHOST BEAT OFF!
HEE, HEE!

-SNFF- AH... AH'M REAL SORRY, AKI! KIN AH REALLY STAY ...?

SURE! WELL, FOR A WHILE, AT LEAST!
IT'S JUST A STUDIO APART-MENT, YOU KNOW...

AH... AH'M *POWERFUL* OBLIGED T' YUH...
snff

OKAY, I'M OFF TO *WORK.*

I WON'T BE BACK UNTIL AFTER MIDNIGHT...
...SO DON'T WAIT UP FOR ME.
AH FEEL JEST AWFUL, AKI!

HERE Y'ARE, WORKIN' SO HARD, AND AH'M JEST SITTIN' AROUND... 'TAIN'T RIGHT!

IT'S NO PROB, HARUO, REALLY!
SEE YOU LATER!

FWASH

HEBA! HAVE FUN!
EPISODE 5
GOTTA GET ME A JOB!

BTAM

I CAN'T JUST MOOCH OFF AKI FOREVER.
I'VE *GOTTA* GET ME A *JOB...* SOMEHOW...

WITH TWO STRAIGHT WINS, KŌJI URYŪ HAS SET A BLISTERING PACE SINCE THE SEASON OPENER! AND TODAY HE'S DOING IT AGAIN...
...HOLDING THE FORMIDABLE KINTETSU LINEUP TO NO HITS, BOTTOM OF THE FOURTH!
SEIBU

VOOOSHH
yay!
STRIKE THREE! HE'S OUT!! AND SO, AS WE HEAD INTO THE FIFTH, SEIBU LEADS THREE-NOTHING!

I CAIN'T JEST SIT AROUND LAIK A BUMP ON A LOG!
LEAST I KIN DO IS CLEAN UP A L'IL...

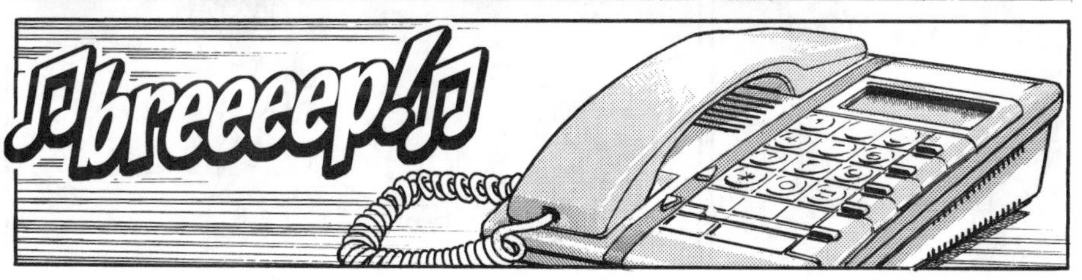
♫breeeep!♫

breeeep!

.....
.....

HELLO ...?

ya-ta-tat-tat!
IIIIT'S T-T-T-Tommy!

....
...!
....
...?

UM... AH'M TERRIBLE SORRY, SIR, BUT IF YER CALLIN' FER AKI....
...SHE'S GONE T' WORK. KIN AH TAKE A MESSAGE, OR--
HUH ?!

SHE'S ON THE JOB TONIGHT?
I'LL HEAD RIGHT ON OVER! THANKS, KID!
KLIK

KSSSHH

....
...?
YA-TA-TAT-TAT!

IIIIT'S ME, "TOMMY-GUN" T-T-T-TOMMY!
AND WHEN I GOTTA GO GO GO... THIS IS THE ONE FOR ME!

....
...!

SKSSHH

SHAKKA

....
...!

....
....

KANGGG
sizzle

MMHHN?

WHOOPS! SORRY 'BOUT THAT, AKI!
GRUB'S ALMOST READY, ANYHOW!
pwheeet!

HARUOOO!! WOULD YOU ***RELAX,*** FOR GOD'S SAKE?!

C'MON! ***LEAST*** I KIN DO...
...IS COOK UP A MESS O' BREAKFAST FER YUH!

THERE! NOW GET THEM GROCERIES DOWN YER NECK QUICK-LIKE OR WE'LL BE LATE FER CLASS!
WOW, LOOKS ***SUPER*** YUMMY!
GEE... IT'S BEEN **YEARS** SINCE I HAD A REAL 'HOMEMADE' BREAKFAST!

UM... AKI?

KIN I ASK YUH A, Y'KNOW... ***PERSONAL*** SORTA QUESTION?
ASK AWAY, GIRL-FRIEND!

AKI...
YER JOB...
IT AIN'T... AH MEAN...

YOU AIN'T SELLING YER BODY ...ARE YUH?

...,
...!

.....
.....

BWA HAW HAW HAW!
HEE HEE HAW KOFF HA HA HA!!
AKIIII!! C'MON, NOW! AH'M SERIOUS!

HARUO, YOU ARE SUCH A HOOT! HOW IN THE HELL DID YOU GET THAT IDEA?!
I MEAN... HA HA HA!

WALL... SEE HERE NOW...
AH BEEN LOOKIN' AROUND FER A PLACE, AND AH KNOW THIS AKASAKA AREA YER IN IS HIGHER 'N HEAVEN FER RENT!
YUH EVEN GOT A VIEW OF TH' TOKYO TOWER!

AH HA HA HA!!
WHEW!

WELL, DON'T WORRY, KID!!
I *DON'T* "SELL MY BODY"... OR EVEN MY *HEART!*
THANK TH' LORD! AH'M PLUMB SORRY FER EVEN *THINKIN'* SECH A THING, AKI!

BUT YUH GOTTA TELL ME! WHAT KINDA WORK *DO* YUH DO THET YOU KIN LIVE LAIK A PRINCESS IN AKASAKA?

I'M A GINZA GIRL!

A... "GINZA GIRL" ...?
???

下鉄
SUBWAY
地下鉄
←AKASAKA

FROM WHUT YER SAYIN', IT JEST SOUNDS LAIK SOME KIND'A FANCY WAITRESS JOB!
WELL, KINDA YES, KINDA NO.
THE WORD WE USE IS HOSTESS.

HUH ...?!

WELL, HECK! THEN MEBBE I KIN DO IT, TOO... Y'THINK?

BUT I CAIN'T JUST TELL MY PORE OL' FOLKS TO SEND ME MORE MONEY SO I KIN MOVE OUT ON MAH OWN. THEY JEST AIN'T GOT IT!
AKI... I CAIN'T GO BACK T' THET HAUNTED ROOM, I JEST CAIN'T!!

I
HEAR
YOU,
GIRL.
BUT...
YOU?
WORK
IN THE
GINZA?

AH AIN'T
NEVER
WORKED
A *REAL*
JOB
BEFORE.
AN' AH HEAR THET
FUYUMI WANTS T' GO
BACK AN' WORK WITH
YUH AG'IN. AH'D
SHORELY FEEL
BETTER WITH
MAH FRIENDS
AROUN'...

....
....

WELL...
IF YOU
INSIST.
NOW I CAN'T
PROMISE
ANYTHING,
BUT I'LL
HAVE A
TALK WITH
OUR
MAMA
AND--

WHUT?!
YER *MA*
WORKS
THERE, TOO?
THET'S
EVEN
BETTER!

....
....

ON SECOND
THOUGHT...
FORGET
I EVEN
MENTIONED
IT.
AH?
AKI!!
WHUT
DID AH
SAY?!
AH'M
SORRY!!

WHEE!! NO WAY! TOO COOL!!
WE'RE ALL GONNA WORK TOGETHER?!

THIS IS JUST SO COOL! IT'LL BE SO MUCH FUN!!
GIRL, YOU'RE GONNA DO JUST FINE!
SO YOU GOTTA PROMISE T' HELP ME OUT!
YUP! I KEP' AT PORE AKI LAIK A HORSEFLY IN SUMMER!

YOU DONE ME A DOUBLE GOOD TURN, AKI!
FUYUMI, YOU CAN START TONIGHT. HARUO, YOU HAVE TO COME BY TOMORROW FOR AN INTERVIEW.
OKAY, YOU TWO! I CALLED MAMA AND SHE SAID SHE CAN USE A COUPLE MORE GIRLS.

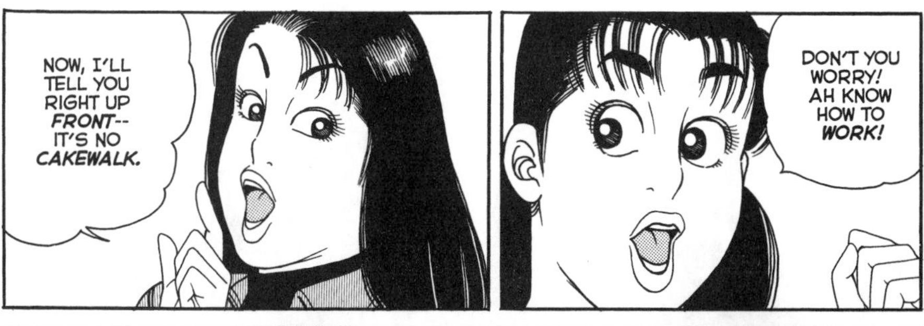
NOW, I'LL TELL YOU RIGHT UP FRONT-- IT'S NO CAKEWALK.
DON'T YOU WORRY! AH KNOW HOW TO WORK!

I LOVE THIS JOB, BUT IT'S NOT FOR EVERYBODY, AND I DO NOT WANT YOU FORCING YOURSELF TO DO IT, HARUO!
TRY IT FOR ONE DAY, AND IF IT'S LIKE, "THIS ISN'T ME" JUST SAY SO, OKAY?

YES, MA'AM!

AWESOME! I'LL WARM UP TONIGHT, THEN TOMORROW YOU AND ME ARE GONNA BLOW SOME MINDS!! ♥
HEE, HEE! PROFESSOR AKI'LL HAVE US IN THE POST-GRAD PROGRAM IN NO TIME!
AH'M COUNTIN' ON YUH!

HOLD IT, YOU TWO! YOU HAVE TO LEARN TO WALK BEFORE YOU CAN RUN!
EH?!

A GINZA GIRL HAS TO REALLY WORK IT! LET 'EM KNOW YOU'RE A BABE!!
SHAKE THAT BOOTY!

LAIK... SO?
OKAY... LEMME SEE...

HANDS LIKE THIS!
LAIK... THIS?
YEAH ...?

BA-BOOM

BOOM BADDA BOOM!

AKI SAID SHE'S WORKIN' SOME KIND O' PARTY TONIGHT, SO GUESS I GOTTA GIT THERE ALL BY MAH LONESOME.

'KAY NOW...
CLUB NINE!

FUJIYA

地下鉄
SUBWAY
銀座駅
Ginza Sta.

新宿駅西口
for Yotsuya-eki

WELL, AH'M A BIG GIRL! AH KIN FIND IT!!
地下鉄
SUBWAY
銀座駅

EPISODE 6
MAH FIRST DAY
A'WORKIN'!

FWHOOSH

ルノアール
2F

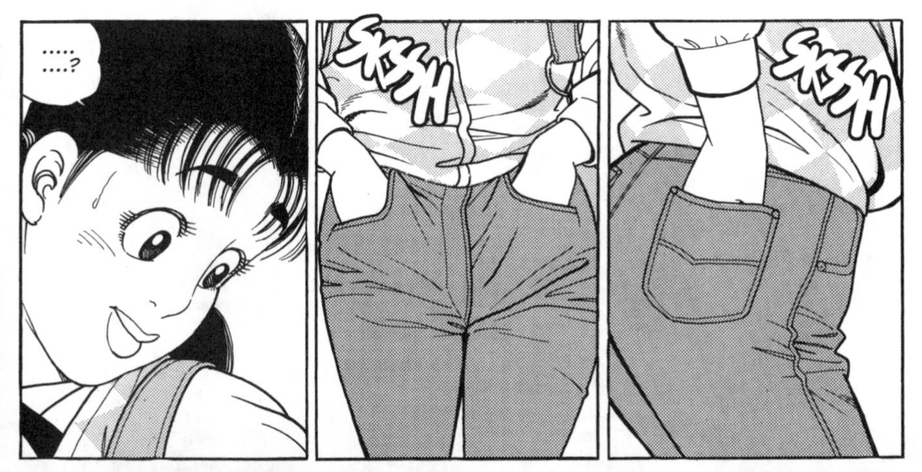
.....
.....?
SWISH
SWISH

.....
.....!
マルコ
2F

.....
.....

AH....
AH LOST
TH' MAP
AN' TH
TELLYPHONE
NUMBER!

GIVE IT UP, SISTER!
I READ SOMEWHERE THERE'S, LIKE, MORE THAN 3,000 CLUBS AROUND HERE!
3,000 ...?! IT...IT CAIN'T BE TRUE!

Kodak
WHAR'S CLUB NINE?!
LOOK, BABE-- I GOT A BETTER IDEA!
FORGET THIS "CLUB NINE" DUMP AND LET'S PARTY AT MY PLACE!
AH DON'T GOT NO TIME FER IT!

'SCUSE ME, BUT--
SIT DOWN, MY DEAR.
PALM READING
THD THD
I SEE... YOU ARE THE YOUNGEST OF THREE GIRLS!
AH'M AN ONLY CHILE!
NOW--KIN YUH HELP ME?! YUH KNOW A PLACE IN THESE HERE PARTS NAME O' "CLUB NINE"...?
NO. BUT YOU ARE TROUBLED BY THREE LOVERS...
THD
SIR! AH'M STILL A VIRGIN!

THD THD THD
OH, LORDY! WHAT KIN AH DO?!
AH PROMISED AKI AH'D BE 'LONG ABOUT SIX!
AN' NOW IT'S COMIN' ON SEVEN!!
THD THD

huff
hahh
hahh
huhh

THD
THD
THD
huff
hahh
hahh
hahh

--WHAT TUH DO!!
AH... AH... AH JEST DON'T KNOW--
大黒屋

club 9nine

BWAHAWHAW!!

NOT LIKE YOU.
GIRLFRIEND, YOU'RE WAY LATE.

I HOPE THAT DIPPY HAYSEED IS OKAY.

CAN'T IMAGINE SHE'D BLOW THIS OFF...

YEEEEOW!!
Chomp

TOMMY!! YOU NUTCASE!! ♥
HOW COME EVERY TIME YOU COME HERE YOU BITE ME?!
'CAUSE NOW YOU GOTTA LET ME GIVE YA A SMOOCH, PRINCESS-- HAIR OF THE DOG THAT BIT YA, GET IT? YA-TA-TAT-TAT!
HEE HEE HEE HEE!

♪breeeep!♫

THANK YOU FOR CALLING CLUB NINE! HOW CAN I HELP YOU...?
HEE HEE! TOMMY, YOU NAUGHTY BOY! YOU KILL ME!

MISS AKI!
PHONE FOR YOU!
THANK GOD! COMING!

CAN'T YOU THINK OF ANYTHING ELSE, TOMMY?
BE BACK IN A SEC!
WHAT'S THE BIG DEAL, AKI? WERE YOU WAITING FOR A CALL FROM YOUR LOVER BOY?

SOMEONE CALLED HARUO HATTORI...?
WHO IS IT?

I KNEW IT!

ACK!
WAAAAAH!!

HELLO? HARUO...?

HA-RU-O!! TAKE A CHILL PILL! I NEED TO KNOW WHERE YOU ARE!
BAWW! WAAH! SOB!

I'VE BEEN WORRIED SICK, HARUO! ARE YOU OKAY?
WH-WHAT'S WRONG?! AND WHERE THE HELL ARE YOU?!

WAAH! MAMA!
BAWWL! AKIIII!
WAAAHN!!
UM, HELLO...? IS THIS AKI SHINOHARA?
I'M CALLING FROM THE SUKIYA STREET *POLICE STATION...*
OH, *NO!!*

NO, DON'T WORRY, MISS-- NOTHING SERIOUS. WE JUST FOUND HER CRYING IN THE STREET.
SHE SAID HER NAME IS HARUO HATTORI AND SHE'D GOTTEN LOST LOOKING FOR A HOSTESS BAR CALLED *CLUB NINE.*
WE FOUND THIS NUMBER IN OUR RECORDS. IS SHE...?
WAAH!! BAWWL!
SNFF

YES, *YES!* SHE'S ONE OF OUR GIRLS!
OH, THANK YOU THANK YOU *THANK YOU!!*
I'LL BE *RIGHT* OVER, SIR! *THANKS AGAIN!!*

MAMA! I HAVE TO TAKE OFF FOR A SEC!
I'VE GOT TO GO PICK UP THAT NEW GIRL I WAS TELLING YOU ABOUT!

PEACHY, DAHLING!
BUT DO RUSH RIGHT BACK!

NOW, TRY NOT TO GET LOST AGAIN-- OKAY, KIDS?
THERE ARE SOME NASTY OL' PEOPLE OUT THERE!

THANKS A LOT, GUYS! SORRY FOR THE TROUBLE!
SNFF SOB
SNFF SOB

玉泉
OH MY GAWD! YOU'VE BEEN WANDERING AROUND FOR THREE HOURS?!

AH JEST DON'T GIT IT! BACK IN AKITA, FOLK'LL JEST TAKE YUH SOMEWHAR IFFEN YUH ASK!
C'MON, HARUO! GET A CLUE! THIS IS THE GINZA, NOT SOME TEENY LITTLE HICK TOWN! NO ONE KNOWS ALL THE CLUBS!

W-WAIT A SEC...
WHAT THE HELL ARE YOU WEARING?!
HUH?! M-MAH BEST WORKIN' CLOTHES!!
YOU'RE GOING TO BE WORKING THE GINZA, NOT SHOVELING COW FLOPS, GIRL! PANTS ARE OUT!
AAAH?! HARUOOO! NO MAKE-UP?!
AW, AKI! I AIN'T EVEN GOT NONE!!
AN' AH ONLY HAD ONE GOOD SKIRT, AND MAH HOUND DOG ATE IT!

WE'RE IN *THAT* BUILDING, NINTH FLOOR!
NINTH FLOOR, CLUB *NINE*... GET IT?
NOW *DON'T* FORGET!
SO *THET'S* THE TRICK...?

.....
.....

club 9 nine

HEE HEE HEE HEE!! snork
OH HOH HOH! OH MY!
TOMMY, DAHLING, DO BEHAVE!
MAMA!
PSST! MAMA!

YES ...?

BTAM

YOUR TURN TO USE THAT SNAZZY NEW TOILET I GAVE YOU GUYS, HUH?! YA-TA-TAT-TAT!
I'M SO SORRY. IF YOU'LL EXCUSE ME A MOMENT...

MAMA, THIS IS THAT NEW GIRL I TOLD YOU ABOUT-- HARUO HATTORI.
AH'M *RIGHT BUSTED* UP 'BOUT BEIN' SO *LATE,* MA'AM!
HELLO, HARUO! WELL, IT SOUNDS TO ME LIKE YOU'RE... ER...FROM *OUT OF TOWN,* SO I CAN UNDERSTAND HOW YOU GOT LOST!

L... LORDY!

IF THAT DON'T BEAT ALL!
MIZ *MAMA,* AH SWEAR YER THE *SPITTIN' IMAGE* A' MAH *REAL* MA!

EHH ...?!

THAT'S *QUITE* IMPOSSIBLE! I'M *HARDLY* OF AN *AGE* TO HAVE *CHILDREN!*
R- REALLY? AH'M *SORRY!*

AND **SO,** HARUO... HOW MANY **REGULAR CUSTOMERS** DO YOU USUALLY BRING IN?
WHAT'S YOUR **MONTHLY TAKE?**
SAY **WHUT?**
OH, MAMA! **SORRY!!**

WHEN I SAID SHE WAS NEW, I MEANT **TOTALLY NEW.**
SHE'S **NEVER** WORKED IN THE BIZ!

FRESH OFF THE FARM, HMM?

WELLL... I DON'T KNOW...

PLEASE, MA'AM! JES' LEMME TRY MAH HAND AT IT!
MY PA ALLUS SAID I TOOK T' WORK BETTER'N ANYONE! AN' AH KIN START THIS VERY **EVE'NIN!**

WELL, IT WOULD BE A **GODSEND,** HEAVEN KNOWS. BUT REALLY... IN **THOSE** RAGS...?
B-BUT THEY'RE ALL AH **GOT!**

AH!!

THAT'S **IT!** THAT **EXQUISITE** LITTLE NUMBER THEY ALL **SO** ADORED AT THAT LAST PARTY!
EH...?

YOU... UH... YOU DON'T MEAN *THIS*...
D-DO YOU?
.....
....!
PICTURE PERFECT, DAHLING! I'LL LET YOU BORROW IT.

.....
.....

M... MIZ MAMA? *YOU* WORE *THET?!*
SO?!
HMPH!

THERE! *THAT'S* DECIDED! NOW LET'S HURRY AND DO THE *REST,* DEAR!
WE'RE BUSY BUSY *BUSY* TONIGHT!
RIGHT! WHEN WE'RE DONE WITH YOU, YOU'LL GIVE YOUR "OL' PA" A *HEART ATTACK!* NOW *STRIP!*

WHTT
FHTT
FSSH
KLIK

TAKK
AWESOME!!
HARUO, YOU ARE TOTALLY CUTE!!
AKI, DAHLING, WE HAVE WORKED ANOTHER CLUB NINE MIRACLE!

SO... HOW OLD ARE YOU, DEAR?
JES' EIGHTEEN, MIZ MAMA!!
EIGHTEEN...
R... REALLY ...?
HOW... NICE. SUCH A NICE AGE.
....?

WHY, COMPARED TO YOU, I...

IN... IN JUST SIXTEEN DAYS...

....
....

....
....

I HATE IT I HATE IT *I HATE IT!* FORTY!
WAAAAH!!
MAMA! THIS IS NO TIME TO *CRY!*
WE'RE "BUSY BUSY *BUSY,*" REMEMBER?!
...
...

KCHAK

Super

A-AKI!! WHUT AM AH SUPPOSED TO DO?!
LORDY, THEY'RE DRUNKER'N PIGS IN THE CIDER MASH!

WELL, FOR STARTERS, SLAP A SMILE ON YOUR FACE, KIDDO!

AND TURN DOWN THE ACCENT A BIT, OKAY?
AH... I GOT YUH!

WHOA! WHO'S THAT LITTLE CUTIE?
OUR NEWEST HEARTBREAKER, GENTLEMEN! AND IT'S HER VERY FIRST DAY!
SO-- DO BE SWEET TO HER!
OH! ISN'T THAT THE DRESS MAMA WAS WEARING LAST...
HEY, IT IS!

OH, MAN, I WAS SHITTING BRICKS THAT NIGHT!
TELL ME ABOUT IT! THE BOSS TOOK ONE LOOK AND TOLD ME IF I EVER INVITED HER AGAIN MY ASS WOULD BE GRASS!
SHHH! SHE'LL HEAR YOU!

HARUOOO! HERE! OVER HERE!
MAN, AM I GLAD TO SEE YOU!

AH'M TERRIBLE SORRY!
AH MISLAID MAH MAP AN' AH GOT LOST AN'...

HARUO, HARUO! YOU'RE SOOO LUCKY!
HE'S HERE!

EH?
WHO'S HERE...?

YOUR RAVE FAVE COMIC-BOOK ARTIST!
MAKOTO KONBAYASHI!!

EH?!

OH, YEAH-- THAT'S **RIGHT!** MAMA, HARUO IS **NUTS** ABOUT THAT COMIC STRIP "WHAT'S BEAR?"...!
HOW **SPLENDID!**
THEN WE SIMPLY **MUST** HAVE HER SIT WITH DEAR **MAKO!**
EHHHH?!

AH... **AH** GITS TO SET NEXT TO M-M-**MAKOTO KONBAYASHI?!**
YOU **HEARD** HER! **GO FOR IT,** KIDDO!

.....
.....!

Konbayashi-Sensei...!!

HNG ...?

THAT... THAT'S **HIM...?**
THE MAN I'VE DREAMED OF MEETING SINCE I WERE A LITTLE TAD...?!

HNGAHH?

.....
.....

KTAK

ARNGGH! FIND MY TOOF! FIND IT!!
IT FELL OUT AGAIN?!
MAAAKOOO! EVERY TIME THIS HAPPENS YOU SWEAR YOU'RE GONNA GO TO THE DENTIST!
.....
.....!

READY, HARUO? GO SIT YOURSELF DOWN!
YES, MAMA!!

AHEM.

SO... WHAZZYER *NAME,* HUH?
AH'M HARUO! HARUO HATTORI!

NICE NAME!
"HER'RO HATTORI."

OH *NO,* SIR! NOT LAIK *THET!* YUH GOTTA SAY IT "HA-*RU*-OH"...!

HE-L'-O...?
UH-UH, NOPE! *HA!! RU!! OH!!*

....
....
....
....

HELLO HATTORI, RIGHT?
NO, SIR!! HA!! RU!! OH!! YOU AIN'T FUNNIN' WITH ME, ARE YUH, SIR?!
OH, IT HARDLY MATTERS, DOES IT?! BESIDES, SHE NEEDS A "WORKING NAME" AND "HELLO" IS SO MUCH EASIER... DON'T YOU THINK?!
HEE HEE! AND IT'S SO CUTE!

HUH...?
YOU'RE SUPPOSED TO LIGHT HIS CIGARETTE!
MATCH!
OH! HARU-- UH, HELLO! MATCH!

HUH ...?
Sktch

OH! OH...! AH GOT IT!

Sktch! Sktch!
AH CAIN'T GIT IT LIT!
Sktch!
Sktch!
Skt FWHSSH

FWTT
OOPS?!

FSSHH

YAIEEEEE!
AH'M SORRY AH'M SORRY AH'M SORRY!!
IS YER COOKIE BRUSH AFIRE?!
WATER!!
WATER NOW!!

EPISODE 7
A LI'L OL' REQUEST FER MISTER KONBAYASHI!

club 9 nine
SKSSSH
club 9 nine
club 9 nine

AH'M TERRIBLE SORRY!
WHADDA YA MEAN, A NATURAL?! LOOK AT MY POOR MUSTACHE!
YES, YES!! YOU'RE A NATURAL!
YEAH! THAT'S IT!!
CLAP CLAP CLAP CLAP CLAP CLAP

SO! INTRODUCTION TIME!
THIS IS MR. KONBAYASHI'S EDITOR, MR. MORIKAWA...
...MR. YURI, THE EDITOR-IN-CHIEF...
AND THE DIRECTOR OF PUBLISHING, MR. YAMANO! ♥
MY PLEASURE!!
MISS HELLO, IS IT? WHAT A CUTE WORKING NAME!

PLEASED T' MEET Y'ALL!
AH'M HARUO HATTORI!
YOU DON'T NEED TO POP UP EVERY TIME, DEAR.

AND THAT CUTE FELLA...
...IS LEWIS ONO, THE CREATOR OF THE MANGA "LONELY BOY."

EH...? YOU DRAW LONELY BOY?!
UH, YEAH.

AH READ THET EV'RY WEEK WHEN IT COMES OUT!! CAIN'T BEAR T' MISS IT!
AN' YOU CAIN'T HARDLY BE ANY OLDER THAN ME, NEITHER! GOL-LEE!

TWENTY YEARS OLD, TWO MILLION A YEAR! ♥
YEESH... ENOUGH TO MAKE YOU PUKE!
LAST YEAR HE'S MY ASSISTANT, CAN'T DRAW WORTH A DAMN, SO I FIRED HIS ASS... AND NOW HE'S PORSCHE BOY!

HEH...NAW, PORSCHES ARE OKAY, BUT I'VE GOT MY SIGHTS ON A TESTA ROSSA.
HELL, IF IT WASN'T FOR TAXES, I COULD BUY ONE NOW. I'M BUSTING MY ASS SO I CAN ORDER ONE NEXT YEAR.
AH JEST KNOW YOU KIN DO IT!!

IFFEN YUH WORK EXTRY HARD...
...AH BET'CHA "LONELY BOY" IS GONNA WIN SOME PRIZE OR SUMTHIN' AND THEN YUH KIN GIT YER PORCH OR TESTEROTTA OR WHATEVER!
UH... THANKS.
?

....
....
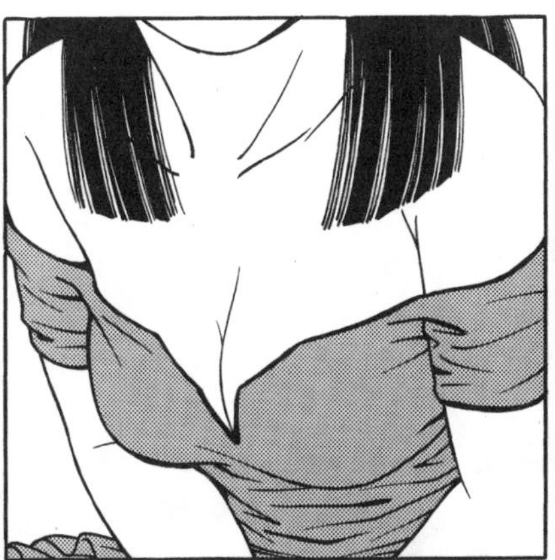

L-LOOKS LIKE SHE'S *AFTER* ME...
UH-OH...
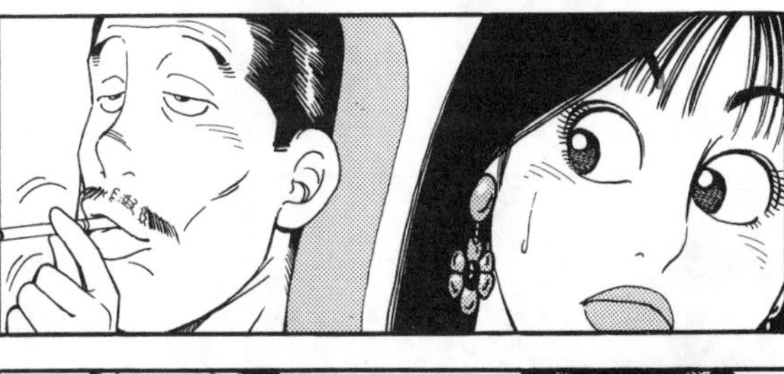

SKSSH

SKSSH

UH, "HELLO"...? I CAN HANDLE THE ONES OVER *HERE.*

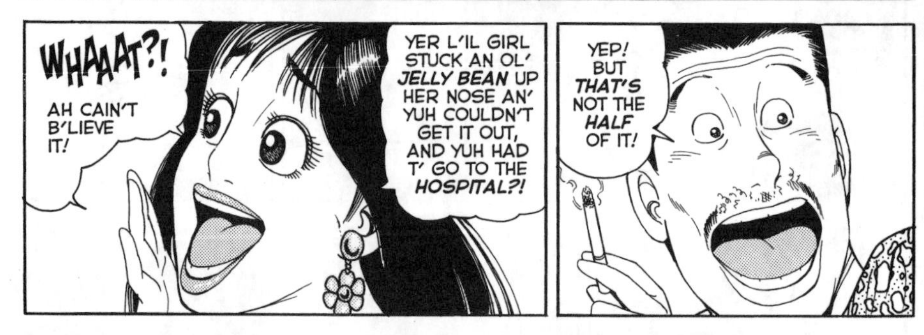
WHAAAT?!
AH CAIN'T B'LIEVE IT!
YER L'IL GIRL STUCK AN OL' *JELLY BEAN* UP HER NOSE AN' YUH COULDN'T GET IT OUT, AND YUH HAD T' GO TO THE *HOSPITAL?!*
YEP! BUT *THAT'S* NOT THE *HALF* OF IT!

NEXT DAY SHE'S SHOWING THE *NEIGHBOR BOY* WHAT HAPPENED... AND GUESS WHAT? THEY *BOTH* GOT THEM STUCK UP THEIR NOSE--*BACK TO THE HOSPITAL!*
BAW HAW HAW HAW HAW!

WAAA HAWW HAWW!!
OH, MY...!
HEE, HEE!

HAHH HAHH HAHH HAHH!

HAHN HAHN HAHN HAHN
....?
....?

HHNN
HHNN
HHNN

HKK
HKK
HKK

HFF
HFF
HFF

.....
.....

HAWF!!!
GASP!!

AH'M SORRY, Y'ALL!
WHEN AH HAS A REAL BELLY LAUGH, SOMETIMES AH FERGITS T' BREATHE!
!!

....
....
SHE'S... C- CUTE.
AW, SHUCKS ...!
SHE'S SOMETHING, ALL RIGHT... LITTLE "MISS HELLO" ...!
HEE HEE!
HARUO, YOU KILL ME!

AKI?
AKI, DEAR!

YOUR HARUO...
...SHE'S REALLY WORKING OUT WELL, ISN'T SHE?

SHE'S CHEERFUL, FRIENDLY, AND CHARISMATIC AS HELL!
SURE IS...!

LIKE I SAID... SHE'S A *NATURAL!*

WELL, WE BETTER HIT THE ROAD, HUH?
RIGHT! THE DEADLINE IS TOMORROW NIGHT-- DON'T BLOW IT!
HEY, TRUST ME, PAL!
UHM... MR. KONBA-YASHI, SIR?
KIN AH ASK YUH ONE L'IL OL' FAVOR?
WHAT IS IT?
AH'D LAIK T' GIT YER AUTO-GRAPH... I'M A POWERFUL BIG FAN, HONEST AN' FER TRUE!
K-KIN YUH DO THET FER ME...?
REALLY TRULY?!
WHEE! I'M ALL OVER HAPPY!
HEY, NO PROB!

AH'LL GO GIT YER A BIT O' PAPER!
NOPE!! I DON'T USE *PAPER.*

EH ...?

SORRY, MISS *HELLO,* BUT HE'S KIND OF A *PRIMA DONNA.* IF YOU WANT AN AUTOGRAPH AND SKETCH YOU'LL JUST HAVE TO GO ALONG WITH HIM.

B... BUT... AH DON'T GIT IT! IF YUH DON'T USE *PAPER,* THEN WHUT...

....
....

HERE!

AWW, BUT HEY!! THET'S NO GOOD!
IFFEN YUH DO IT THAR, IT'LL COME RAHT OFF FIRST TIME AH HAVE ME A BATH!

TOO BAD!
IT'S THERE OR NOWHERE!!
BUT... BUT...!!

COME ON, HARUO! DON'T PITCH A FIT!
YEAH! WE BOTH GOT SIGNED BEFORE YOU GOT HERE!

SEE?
VONBAYASHI
VONBAYASHI

POIK
.....
.....!

THANK YOU SO MUCH!!
DO VISIT US AGAIN!
HEY!! YOU'VE GOT TO WORK TOMORROW NIGHT!
BYE-BYE! SEE YA TOMORROW NIGHT!
2F
B2

MISTER KONBA-YASHI! THANK'EE FER THE AUTOGRAPH AN' L'IL DRAWIN'!
NOW YOU GIT YERSELF T' YER TOOTH DOC RIGHT SHARP!
FOR MARU

IF YOU PRACTICE LIGHTING THOSE MATCHES, FIREBALL!

MISTER LEWIS!! ♥
PLEASE WORK HARD AND BUY A TERRO-RETTA!

UH... YEAH.

....
....

HEY! LEWIS! GET YOUR BUTT IN GEAR!
AH...? YES, SIR!
玉泉堂

PHEWWW!!

GOOD JOB, "MISS HELLO"...! YOU DID GREAT!
AH DID? REALLY TRULY?!
MAH NERVES WAS TWANGIN' LAIK A FIVE-WIRE HORSE FENCE!
YOU ROCKED, GIRL-FRIEND!
THOSE GUYS LOVED YOU TO PIECES!

HMM...
......
FOR MARU
AYASHI

FOR MARU
AYASHI

DEAR MARU... I WONDER HOW MY OLD HOUND DOG IS DOING... BACK IN AKITA?
I'M TRYING MY BEST HERE IN THE BIG CITY, MARU...!
FOR MARU
AYASHI

AKI!
AKI, HON!
CAN I TRUST HER?
SHE WON'T JUST TAKE MY MONEY AND RUN, WILL SHE?
HUH?

DON'T WORRY, MAMA!
THAT GIRL REDEFINES THE WORD "HONEST" ...!

REALLY?!

IN THAT CASE... MISS HELLO, DAHLING? COME ON WITH ME!
YES, MA'AM !!

NOW... YOU PART-TIME GIRLS WORK BY THE HOUR, YOU SEE.
PLUS COMPANION BONUS, SECTION BONUS... HMM...
MA'AM ...?

ADD THEM ALL *UP*... AND *HERE'S* YOUR SHARE. WELL...?

.....
.....!

B-BUT THIS HERE *CAIN'T* BE RAHT! I MEAN... *LORDY,* MAMA!
IT'S MOR'N MAH PORE OL' PAPA MAKES IN A WHOLE *WEEK!*
FOR MARU
AND YOU CAN MAKE *FAR MORE* THAN *THAT* IF YOU *TRY*, DEAR.
AFTER ALL, THIS IS THE *GINZA*-- THE WORLD'S *PRICIEST* ENTER-TAINMENT DISTRICT!

NOW, *OBVIOUSLY* YOU HAVE NO MONEY FOR *CLOTHES.*

HERE-- GO BUY YOURSELF SOMETHING *APPROPRIATE* FOR A *GINZA GIRL.*
NO *JEANS,* NO *SLACKS,* NO *KNITS*-- UNDER-STAND?

B-BUT MAMA! AH CAIN'T TAKE ALL THIS HERE--
OH, DON'T WORRY, DAHLING... I'LL TAKE IT OUT OF YOUR SALARY.

BUT STARTING TODAY, YOU'RE A REAL GINZA GIRL!
YOU'VE GOT TO LOOK SHARP AND KEEP THOSE CUSTOMERS COMING BACK!

Y-YES, MA'AM!
AH'LL GET DECKED UP PROPER!

HI, I'M CHINATSU.
I'M A NEW PART-TIMER, JUST LIKE YOU. WE CAN BACK EACH OTHER UP!

MUCH OBLIGED, CHINATSU!
THET'S GREAT!

I'M RUMI.
IF YOU NEED A HAND WITH ANYTHING, JUST ASK.
I'M YUKI.
KIYOKO!
AND I'M KYOKO ...!
PLEASED T' MEET Y'ALL!

WE ARE... GINZA GIRLS!

NOW, LADIES! WE HAVE TO WELCOME MISS HELLO PROPERLY-- LET'S GO OUT FOR UDON!
I KNOW THE TASTIEST PLACE ON THE GINZA!
YAHOO!
LET'S GO, LET'S GO!

BEGGIN' YER PARDON, MIZ MAMA...

THANK YOU KINDLY FER THE LOAN OF THIS HERE FINE DRESS!
I'LL GIT IT DRY-CLEANED IT AND BRING IT RAHT BACK!
FOR MARU

....
....

HMPH!!
THAT OLD THING...? YOU CAN HAVE IT.

WELL, DAHLINGS?! LET'S SASHAY!!

HERE-- YOU BETTER BORROW MINE.
YOU CAN'T WALK AROUND LIKE *THAT!*
THANK'EE, AKI!

EPISODE 8
A FAREWELL TO GHOSTS

YER A GHOST. Y'ALL MIND NOT HAUNTIN' THE PLACE IN BROAD DAYLIGHT?!
YOU'RE REALLY GOING TO LEAVE ME?

IT WAS A JILLION LAUGHS, BUT NOW AH'M OUTTA HERE.
HEBA!

....
....

BUT... I'M STILL A VIRGIN!

AH'M PLUMB CERTAIN THET THERE PLACE'LL BE JAM FULL O' CUTER GIRLS THAN ME!
WOULD YUH PLEASE JEST GIT ON UP T' HEAVEN?!

....
....
FSSSSSH
DO YEW MIND?!
SLAM

....
....

WHUT?! YUH LEFT TH' DORM?!
マルの家
SORRY, PA! BUT I JEST HAD T' MOVE!
AND AH ALREADY GOT ME AN APARTMENT AN' A PART-TIME JOB AN' ALL! PLEASE DON'T BE MAD OR NUTHIN', PAPA!
WULL... IF YER SURE YER OKAY... AH GUESS YER A BIG GIRL...
ANYHOW, THANGS ARE IN A SERIOUS KERFUFFLE DOWN HOME HERE.

OH, NO! WHUT HAP- PENED?
WHAT'S TH' KER- FUFFLE ABOUT?

.....
.....

YER MA AND I...WE HAD A BIT O' A SQUABBLE.

EHHH?!
ABOUT WHAT?!

AW, NUTHIN'. YUH AIN'T MARRIED... YUH WOULDN'T UNDERSTAND.

NO FAIR! TELL ME, PAPA!
AH AIN'T NO SPRAT NO MORE!

....
....

I WAS CHOWIN' DOWN, COUPLE A' DAYS AGO...

♪ LIKE A VIRGIN... ♪
KSSH

TAH!! TAH!!
FAP FAP

YA TA TATTA TATTA...

LIKE A VIRRRR-GIN...

!!
WHAM
AH'VE HAD ENOUGH O' THAT, WOMAN!

EEK!
GIT YER BUTT OVER HERE!

FAP FAP
FAP

YEAH, AH KNOW I OUGHTN'T A' SMACKED HER...
BUT DAG NABBIT! SHE'S BEEN A' SMACKIN' ME FER WEEKS!
....
....
AH SEE. SO...
WHUT HAP-PENED NEXT?

NEXT...
GRRR!! AH DIDN'T SMACK YEW THREE TIMES!!
WHAPPITY
WHAPPITY
WHAPPITY
WHAPPITY
WHAPPITY
WHAPPITY
WHAPPITY
WHAPPITY
WHAPPITY
WHAPPITY

...AND SHE AIN'T SPOKE A WORD T' ME SINCE.
UH-HUH.
YOU TWO MAKE UP NOW, Y'HEAR?

THAR!!
EVERY-THIN'S ALL SPICK AND SPAN!

WELL, AH'M *REALLY* OUT ON MAH OWN, NOW!
LORDY, I DUNNO *HOW* I'LL MAKE OUT, WHAT WITH SCHOOL *AND* WORK...
BUT AH AIN'T *NEVER* BEEN A QUITTER!
AN' NOW... MAH BESTEST THING! ♥

HEBA!! AH'VE GOT TO SKINNY OFF T' WORK NOW, KINGORO, DARLIN'! AH MAY COME HOME WITH THE OWLS, BUT YEW GOTTA WAIT UP FER ME, Y'HEAR? ♥

NEC
HONK
BRMBB

CHENAL

SO! WHAT LOOK ARE YOU AFTER...?
LESSEE... HMM...

WEL-COME TO CHENAL, MY DEAR! ♥

KIN Y'ALL RIG ME UP LIKE A PROPER *GINZA GIRL?*

WHY, DARLING, THAT'S OUR *SPECIALTY!*

HOW I DO EET, *MADEMOISELLE?*

AH WANTS T' LOOK LIKE A *GINZA GIRL!*
....
...!

TA-
DAH!

BOOM
BADDA
BOOM!

WHOA! WHO'S THE SEXY LADY?
A FRIEND OF YOURS ...?
I WISH! NEVER SEEN HER BEFORE!

HMM...?

H-HEY! GRANPAW! WAKE UP!!
YER GONNA SET YERSELF AFIRE!

WATCH YER BUTT!
YER GONNA--

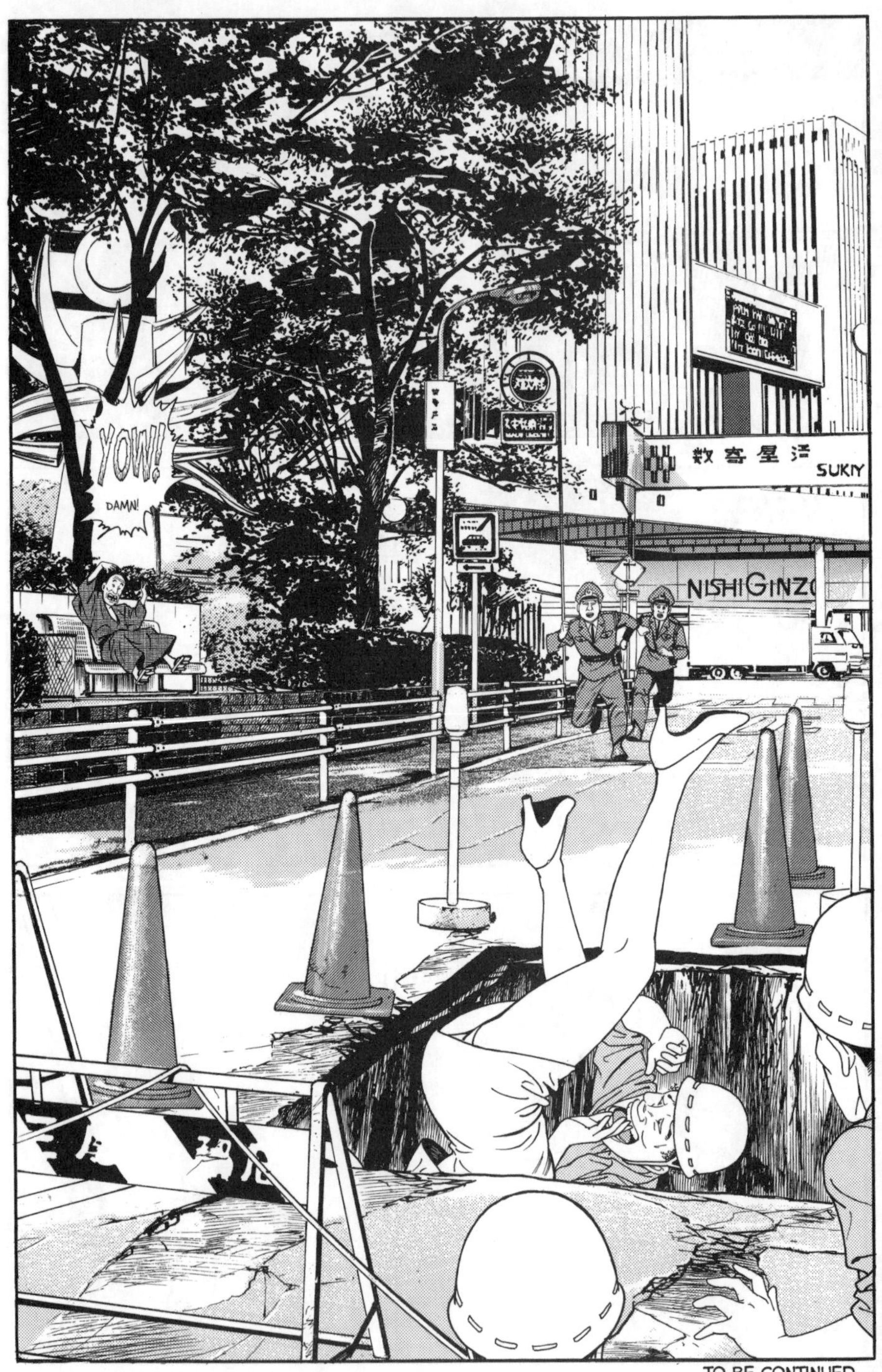

TO BE CONTINUED...

BONNIE AND CLYDE
ISBN: 1-56971-215-8 $13.95

MISFIRE
ISBN: 1-56971-253-0 $14.95

THE RETURN OF GRAY
ISBN: 1-56971-299-9 $17.95

GOLDIE VS. MISTY
ISBN: 1-56971-371-5 $15.95

BAD TRIP
ISBN: 1-56971-442-8 $13.95

BEAN BANDIT
ISBN: 1-56971-453-3 $16.95

KIDNAPPED
ISBN: 1-56971-529-7 $16.95

MISTER V
ISBN: 1-56971-550-5 $18.95

MISTY'S RUN
ISBN: 1-56971-684-6 $14.95

ACTION FIGURES
RALLY #10-066
MINNIE-MAY #10-073
$13.99 EACH!

LIMITED-EDITION STATUE
#19-168 $150.00

KENICHI SONODA

GUNSMITH ガンスミスキャッツ CATS

To find a comics shop in your area, call 1-888-266-4226

For more information or to order direct: •On the web: www.darkhorse.com •E-mail: mailorder@darkhorse.com
•Phone: 1-800-862-0052 or (503) 652-9701 Mon.-Sat. 9 A.M. to 5 P.M. Pacific Time

Prices and availability subject to change without notice.